# Hunting Fish

# Hunting Fish

A Cross-Country Search
For America's Worst Poker Players

## Jay Greenspan

St. Martin's Press
New York

www.stmartins.com

Library of Congress Cataloging-in-Publication Data

Greenspan, Jay, 1968–
    Hunting fish : a cross-country search for America's worst poker players / Jay Greenspan.—1st ed.
        p. cm.
    ISBN-13: 978-0-312-34783-3
    ISBN-10: 0-312-34783-9
    1. Poker. I. Title

GV1251.G777 2006
795.412—dc22

                                                                        2006041724

First Edition: August 2006

10  9  8  7  6  5  4  3  2  1

# CONTENTS

# ACKNOWLEDGMENTS

IT TOOK NEARLY TWO YEARS TO COMPLETE THIS BOOK, AND in that time I've relied on the generosity of dozens of wonderful people. As I traveled across the country, I was invited into homes and clubs where I was treated warmly. To protect the anonymity of those who shared their tables with me, I changed the names of most of the players I encountered. Still, I need to thank you all. You were wonderful hosts.

Kevin Factor, Dan Michalski, Steve Clancy, and Carol Schmidt (a.k.a. Mom) provided critical feedback at various points in the writing of the book. Without their close readings and intelligent critiques, this book would be far less than it currently is.

My interest in poker would have waned long ago had I not started my education with a group of thoughtful New Yorkers with whom I've been trading theories and hand histories for years. Thanks to Derek Mithaug, Alex Naro, Eric "Double Double" Lindnauer, and Josh "Kid Dynamite" Kattef for sharing their thoughts and humor. Over the last few years, Greg Ecker has become a trusted advisor and close friend. Also thanks to the Pokersavvy.com forums.

I. Nelson Rose, Jonathan Grotenstein, and Howard Schwartz at the Gambler's Book Shop in Las Vegas helped with research of various portions of the book.

I will forever be indebted to Greg Dinkin and Frank Scantoni of Venture Literary for their work in developing this project. Their assistance was vital at every stage, from the development of the concept to the completion of the manuscript.

Marc Resnick and the team at St. Martin's displayed an inspiring level of talent and thoughtfulness. Thank you all for your help.

I don't know how to properly thank Marisa for her support and love and patience, so I'll keep it simple: Thanks, sweetie. I love you.

# Hunting Fish

# PROLOGUE

C*ALM, STAY CALM,* AN INNER VOICE PLEADED. THE LOSS
wasn't the largest I'd taken in one shot, and succumbing to panic
wouldn't help anything. But the calls for reason couldn't stem the
rush of dread and anger flooding my head.

"*Fuck!*" I screamed. I paced the room and punched a coat,
sending it flying off the rack.

Marisa, my fiancée, studied me with a mixture of concern and
fascination. In the time we'd been together, almost three years,
she'd never witnessed one of my fits. With the help of a decent
therapist, I'd learned how reason could overtake the instincts that
create those episodes. My losing battle for control revealed an aspect of my character she'd never seen before.

*Don't subject her to this, Jay,* the inner voice continued. *And don't
embarrass yourself. Remember what Dr. Hermann said: "Work pragmatically with the situation. Deal only with what you can."*

What was the situation and what could I do? Overnight, while
Marisa and I slept in the bottom floor of our Brooklyn duplex,
someone had broken in through our kitchen window. My wallet,
my cell phone, and seventeen hundred–dollar bills were gone.

"*Fuck. Fuck. Fuck!*"

Just weeks earlier, a trusting editor had bought a proposal I'd written for a chronicle of a three-month cross-country poker journey. The schedule was brutally tight, and I was supposed to start my trip in two weeks. But as of that morning, I had no driver's license, no credit cards, no ATM cards.

*"Motherfucker."*

Everything would need to be replaced. Including the money. I'd been losing, on a really nasty run of cards, and my bankroll was getting frightfully low. Now, without playing a single hand of poker, I'd lost another $1,700.

The book, as I pitched it, was supposed to be the story of my attempts to move from the medium stakes, where I might win or lose as much as $1,000 or $1,500 on a night, to the high stakes, where the swings could be a few thousand on a single hand. But with the ungodly run I was on, my bankroll was quickly becoming insufficient for even the middle-level stakes I was playing. If the cold streak continued much longer, I'd have to drop down and play smaller just to make sure I didn't go broke. I guessed that neither my editor nor the poker-reading public would be especially interested in tales of $75 wins and $50 losses. No, if the book was going to be even moderately compelling, I'd need to start winning. And soon.

*Get your shit together,* the voice screamed. Finally, I listened.

"It's fine, sweetie." I managed. "It's fine. Guess I should call the credit card companies."

She nodded.

*"Shit!"*

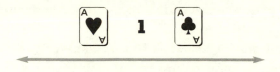

# FOXWOODS

Call," I said, and placed the red $5 chip in front of my cards. I generally don't like limping under the gun—usually it's raise or fold—but what are you going to do with pocket 9s? Some of the books, the bad ones, would say I should just fold this hand. Those novice manuals preach the power of the highest-quality starting hands—pocket Aces, Kings, and Queens—especially when out of position, but I'd long since decided that about three-quarters of the available no-limit hold 'em literature was crap, encouraging a style of play as predictable as it was tedious. No, I was playing these cards, no question about that. In fact, to my way of thinking, pocket 9s was just about the perfect hand for the situation.

I was at Foxwoods, the mammoth Indian casino in eastern Connecticut that was my first stop on the trip, playing $5-$5 no-limit hold'em. They don't cap the buy-in at Foxwoods, so I was playing with $1,200 on the table in a mix of chips and cash, but I wasn't even close to the deepest stack. Across the table, a stocky bald man had a wad of $100s—must have been eight or nine thousand—folded in half and held together by a couple of rubber bands. To my right, a sixty-year-old with the hair and face of a former drill sergeant kept about $5,000 in front of him, and two seats to my left, a fiftyish Bostonian with a head of thick, wavy gray hair and a paunch that pressed into his polo shirt, had about four grand.

The drill sergeant, Baldy, and I, the good players at the table, had watched the Bostonian throw heaps of money into pots with nothing more than second pair or a gutshot draw, but he was on a rush, hitting everything—nailing trips on the turn, filling in the straight on the river. It couldn't continue, though. We knew that. If he kept putting his money in on draws, he'd go broke. It was a certainty.

I hadn't exchanged a word with the other good players at the table, but we recognized each other's skill and stayed out of each other's pots. Of course, if the cards required it, we'd do battle. We weren't playing as a team or colluding in any way, but there was an easy mark at the table. There was no need to take on a good player when a fish of this size was around.

"Raise," announced the Bostonian. "Twenty-five." He threw out a green chip.

Perfect. When I called with pocket 9s I was actually hoping to get raised. I wanted someone else to start with a strong hand, something I could topple if the flop hit me. Baldy and the drill sergeant folded. It was my turn to try and land this tuna.

The small blind called, as did I.

The dealer put down a flop of J♠-9♠-4♥. (See Fig. 1.)

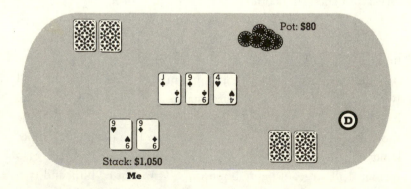

Pot: $80

Stack: $1,050

**Me**

I hit it—my set of 9s, the one on the board matching the two in my hand. I now had the second nuts—the second-best possible hand given the board. Only pocket Jacks would have been a favorite over me at that point, and if someone had that—well, I was just going to go broke.

I prayed that my fish held Ace-Jack or pocket Kings, something he wasn't close to having the discipline or skill to fold.

The small blind checked.

I bet. "Fifty," I announced.

"Raise," the fish replied. "One-fifty."

To my shock the small blind then called and reluctantly tossed out six green chips.

Suddenly my hand seemed vulnerable. With two spades on the flop and that kind of betting, I could be pretty sure that one of my opponents had two spades in the hole. If another spade appeared on the turn or river, my set would lose to a flush. If either one of them was going to hit their draw, they were going to pay for it.

"Six hundred." I said. I didn't reach for my chips here. Instead, I picked up my pile of bills and counted out the proper amount.

They'd barely hit the felt when the Bostonian fish called. A quick call after that kind of raise: I knew exactly what he had, a flush draw. A fish doesn't fold a flush draw.

The small blind folded. The turn was the highly innocuous 2♦.

"All-in," I said, and pushed the remaining $400 into the pot.

"Call."

The river was the 5♠.

The fish then showed his hole cards—A♠-10♠. He rivered the Ace-high flush and took the $2,500 pot.

This was an unfortunate end, but the fact that I lost over $1,100 on this hand and another $1,500 on a similar one a couple of hours later was nearly irrelevant. I played well. I did the right things and I got unlucky. It happens all the time in poker. I needed to shake it off, put some more money on the table, and play the next hand with the same acuity I played this one. That's what my detached peers on the Internet discussion boards would write. That's what all the books say.

There was just one problem: After dropping $2,500 only four hours into my three-month trip, I was a panicky, frazzled mess.

For the preceding weeks, it didn't seem to matter what hole cards I had or how hard I hit a flop. I was destined to lose. Flush under flush, set under set, runner-runner draws—I'd seen them all in the last month. As much as I realized stretches like this were inevitable and that my luck would eventually turn, I was scared. I could be in the midst of an epic swing that would run through my entire bankroll. Most players, including top pros, tell of cold streaks that lasted six months, and almost every pro has gone broke at least a couple of times.

I was thirty-six as I walked through Foxwoods' corridors that winter day, and recently engaged. In the easily remembered past, I had a fulfilling, reasonably lucrative career as a technology writer. Yet somehow I'd manipulated my life so that financial disaster had become a distinct possibility.

Foxwoods is not a soothing setting when one is feeling frightened and overwhelmed. The place is monstrous, the largest casino in the world. Its proximity to New York, Boston, and the rest of New England makes it the most convenient destination for millions of gamblers. The uninspired architecture and lazy interior design reflect both the breadth of Foxwoods' player pool and the lack of competition. The hallways are underlit and endless. The walk from one end of the space to another takes nearly half an hour, more if you get lost. The walls are an ashy color and stretch forty feet high. In early December, when I was there, cold Connecticut air circulated through the halls with surprising force.

The food is disgusting. And expensive.

Fortified with a Nathan's hot dog and wishing for a thicker jacket, I walked laps around one of the slot rooms, trying to calm myself. I was still OK. I had to keep telling myself that. My bankroll had taken a beating, for sure, but I wasn't that close to broke. I had a bankroll that could handle losses like this.

On the way to my hotel room, I stumbled upon an upscale jeweler. I looked in the window, and the glitter of the gold and diamonds brought another pressing problem to the fore: I had to buy a ring.

Marisa agreed to be my wife shortly before this trip started, but my proposal was not accompanied by a ring. I wanted her involved in the shopping process, as I have little confidence in my taste in jewelry. My reasoning was sensible enough, I think. She has to wear this thing for the rest of her life, so she might as well like it. The brief time we had to shop before I started the trip went poorly. A sales clerk in Fortunoff's, a ritzy jewelry store on Fifth Avenue, became frustrated with our you-must-be-fucking-kidding-me looks upon seeing price tags, and told us we "don't have a clue." We agreed.

When we announced our happy news over Thanksgiving weekend, our families asked innumerable questions about the conspicuously missing ring. Though Marisa appeared truly indifferent to the nature of her diamond and seemed as horrified as I at the potential cost, there was pressure. Marisa's Aunt Lois, I quickly learned, is something of a gem expert. She had recently helped her son buy a ring for his charming fiancée, and as she discussed the various cuts and qualities Marisa should be concerned with, it became clear that if I scrimped on even one of the four c's, it would be noticed. If I wanted to start off well in this family, I needed to buy a good rock.

A couple of weeks earlier, before my cold stretch started, I could have peeled twenty to forty hundred-dollar bills off my roll and handed them to a Hasid on Forty-seventh Street, who would ensure that I was getting the best deal since the Louisiana Purchase, but that wasn't an option anymore. I needed that money for my bankroll.

I tried to be philosophical about the delay in the ring purchase.

Poker, for me, was something of a business. An idiotic business, it seemed right then, but a business nonetheless. And at that moment, I was undercapitalized—had a negative cash flow. I couldn't be expected to cut into my operating capital at such a time. That would be foolish. Everyone could understand that.

I kept repeating some version of this argument to myself because, if I allowed my thoughts to wander, I might conclude that I'd given up a profitable career to become a professional gambler and—surprise, surprise!—it was going so poorly that I couldn't buy my love an engagement ring.


Greg Raymer was the reigning world champion of poker when I visited him during my Foxwoods trip. In May of 2004, he bested a field of 2,576 entrants to win the $10,000 buy-in no-limit hold 'em event of the World Series of Poker, taking a staggering $5 million. ESPN chronicled his sharp, aggressive play and great luck as he plowed through player after player. A heavy man in his late thirties with a receding hairline, Greg was even-keeled and amiable throughout the event. He seemed to have kind words and a handshake for everyone.

Greg, his wife, and daughter live in a gray colonial-inspired house that sits alongside a wooded road only five miles from Foxwoods. The house is awkwardly large for the lot and sits a bit too close to the road. The term "McMansion" seems apt, and I imagine some of his neighbors in the decades-old homes down the street protested the zoning when his house and a couple of others were built a few years back.

The interior was tasteful, decorated with antiques that Greg and his wife had gathered from estate sales. As Greg and I talked about the furniture and his life, my ring dilemma somehow came up, and he mentioned that I might be able to find a nice engagement ring fairly cheap at an estate sale.

The price of things recurred in our conversation, and it was clear that, despite his windfall, Greg was well aware of the costs of living well and the ease with which money could be squandered.

He'd been playing poker for twelve years before his big win. At the start of his poker career, he was living in Southern California and playing occasionally at the low-limit tables at the casinos around San Diego. He was intrigued with the game, but his wife was concerned with his hobby. She felt poker was like craps or slots—a guaranteed loser. Greg added, "She felt poker was gambling. Gambling led to addiction; addiction led to bankruptcy and ruination of the family." To assure her, he made a deal. He took $1,000 and devoted that to poker. If he lost it, he told his wife, he'd quit the game.

It was a healthy and reasonable compromise, and one that worked out extraordinarily well. As a patent attorney working in the pharmaceutical industry, Greg made a healthy income, and he was able to supplement it with poker winnings. Over the years, as the stakes he played increased, poker funded vacations and other discretionary purchases. When his family moved to Connecticut, the proceeds from a tournament win helped them get a more favorable rate on their mortgage as they increased their down payment.

Usually gambler's tales highlight extravagance or depravity. In gambling lore, big wins are inevitably followed by absurdly wasteful expenditures, and losses are of staggering and disastrous sums. In a way, this makes perfect sense. To be great, a player must have a huge tolerance for risk; he must be at least a little reckless. That way, when all is going well—when the player properly weighs potential outcomes and statistical likelihoods play out as expected—he ensures himself the highest possible return. Of course, when things are going poorly—when the player makes flawed analyses, or when statistical anomalies occur—his riches will quickly disappear. A three-time winner of the World Series main event who reportedly had won approximately $30 million gambling, the great Stu Ungar died penniless. Nick "the Greek" Dandalos, one of the legendary figures of modern poker, a man who'd won millions and played Doyle Brunson and Johnny Moss for the highest stakes, spent his final years playing $5 games in Gardenia. I've seen Huck Seed, another world champion, playing $5-$10 7-stud in an attempt to gather enough for a tournament buy-in. Of course, not all players squander their winnings, but Raymer may be the first determined gambler in history whose winnings were used to avoid what he called "near usurious interest rates."

Which is to say that even in the wake of his seven-figure take, Raymer has a sober and practical view of the future. He was taking advantage of his celebrity by receiving appearance fees at a variety of events. But he realized that in just a matter of months, there would almost certainly be another champion, and his celebrity would quickly pass.

He had no plans on becoming a full-time pro. An experienced lawyer in a sought-after specialty, he didn't see how he could make the same living playing poker that he could in law.

Plus, he noted that when he returned to law full-time, he could be a special asset to some firm. While recruiting a big client, the senior partners might be able to entice an executive to a round of golf by filling out the foursome with a World Series of Poker champion.

At the start of the trip, I'd been playing semiprofessionally for almost two years. Unencumbered by a car, house, or loans, medium-stakes poker provided a decent living and an enviable lifestyle. I played poker and wrote about playing poker. With only the occasional deadline to concern myself with, I could go weeks without encountering anything that might be deemed an obligation. I managed to keep up with the rent and pay for the occasional vacation.

This wasn't sustainable. Marisa and I will start a family before long. For this portion of my life—the remaining forty or fifty years—I wanted a more Raymer-like existence, complete with the luxuries and securities a legitimate career affords, but I wasn't about to give up on poker. I love this game, and I could make enough money, I thought, if I could beat higher-stakes games, where my earnings could support an upper-middle-class lifestyle.

The $10-$20 no-limit at Commerce Casino in Los Angeles was such a game. I'd stand to win or lose $5,000 or more in a session there, with a potential annual income well beyond $100,000, but the players at that level would be tougher. To find out if I could beat the guys who regularly played for high stakes, I'd need a deep bankroll—at least $35,000. After the recent losses, I only had about $15,000.

The book deal gave me a three-month window and an expenses-paid cross-country journey during which I had nothing to do but travel and attempt to pad my roll. In that time, if things went well, I could make the $20,000 that would allow me to take a shot at the Commerce game. It was an ambitious goal at the stakes I was playing, and given how things had been going, a win of that magnitude seemed absurd.

Going into my second session at Foxwoods, I couldn't worry about my career path within the game or what I'd do if I failed to meet my goal.

It was possible. I could make $20,000 in three months. I had to believe that.


On my second day at Foxwoods, there were no fish at the table, nobody splashing money in pot after pot, but there were a couple of weak players and a kid—he couldn't have been more than twenty-two—whom I thought I could take advantage of. The kid wore a Yankees cap and a loose-fitting dress shirt. He had a huge sum of money in front of him—close to $4,000 dollars. I could

tell by his continual smirk that he'd won most of it. He was playing cocky, involving himself in a ton of hands and trying to take
down about every pot with a moderate-sized bet.

It was working. Several times someone would bet, the kid would
make a small raise, and the opponent would fold. Or the kid would
make a small bet at a pot, and watch as everyone else surrendered. It
was bizarre. I couldn't figure out why they were showing him such
deference.

About twenty minutes into the session I was in early position
(in the seats immediately to the left of the blinds) and I raised to
$25 with Ace-King. The kid, who had the button, called. The
flop was J♥-7♠-4♥. (See Fig. 2.)

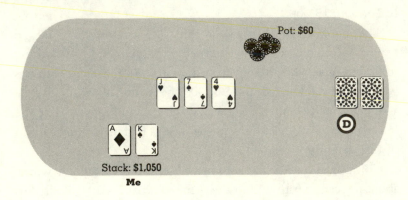

A complete miss for me. I had no pair and no draw, but I'll often follow up a preflop raise with a bet on the flop. The hope is
that the opponent missed the flop as well, and is willing to let the
hand go and surrender a small pot. So I tossed out $50. The kid
raised to $100.

Bets and raises are a means of conversation at a no-limit hold
'em table. A bet tells an opponent that you think you have the best
hand. A raise of that initial bet is a reply saying something like,
"You think you're good, but you're wrong; I've got something

better than you." Of course, a message can be intended to deceive, but the language is the same.

The size of bets is what gives the conversation its specificity. In this case, a raise to $100—a simple doubling of my bet—showed a real lack of confidence. If he had put out, say, $150 or $200, the message would have been "I'm strong here. Put in money at your own risk." I thought he was weak when he made these small raises in the past, and I wasn't about to change my interpretation of his betting language here. To me, the $100 bet said something like "I have a hand that I think might be good, but I'm really not sure. What do you think?"

I think, *Fuck your weak-ass bet.* "Three-seventy-five," I announced.

He nodded and mumbled, "Now that's a raise." Then he folded.

The next hand against him went similarly. Later, I took another $600 from him when I allowed him to make his weak bet into my full house.

I left up about $800 for the day.


The dealers at Foxwoods may be the worst of any major casino in the United States. As a group, they are distracted and slow. On my third day at Foxwoods, during one half-hour period (for which the players pay $6 for the seat), we saw a total of eight hands. I was card dead that day—unable to find a decent starting hand—and the tedium was wearing on me.

My table offered an interesting mix of total fish and highly skilled players. The young guy to my immediate left was extremely aggressive, and willing to let go of a lot of chips on very little. He didn't mind the huge fluctuations in his stack, and it was making my life difficult as he either raised or reraised any pot I entered. I fought back a bit—made a couple of oversized reraises when I felt he had gotten out of line—and that got him off my back for a while.

The most interesting spectacle this day concerned the flirtations between a tall, homely man in his midforties and the woman to his left, who must have been twenty-five years his senior. They joked, sharing small laughs; he leaned into her space to peer at her hole cards; his arm reached briefly around her shoulders on a couple of occasions. I shouldn't have found the sight as unsettling as I did.

Two hours into the session, the woman hit a three-outer against me in a $1,200 pot. The man gave her a high five and they whooped in unison. I thought they might kiss. I then made a comment about their lack of manners. The deserved winner of the pot, I pointed out, was a mere ten feet away, and he was a little upset with the outcome. Maybe their celebration was a bit insensitive.

"I don't fucking care," the man shot back, with the typical Bostonian disdain for the letter *r*. "What are we, at the fucking Harvard Club?"

I got back to work and managed a $900 win for the day. I felt fortunate to be leaving Foxwoods down less than a grand.

# PHILADELPHIA

**A**NY DECENT BEGINNER'S HOW-TO BOOK ON POKER WILL take time in the early chapters to discuss the importance of a bankroll. That explanation usually describes the bankroll as a cache of money that is segregated from other accounts. By keeping this sum apart from the money that is used for bills or savings or discretionary expenses, the player safeguards himself against his own propensity for incaution and stupidity. If the player takes this advice seriously, his foray into poker may be brief and unpleasant, but it won't be life altering.

I hadn't done any reading prior to my first ventures in casino poker. I was living in San Francisco at the time, and made occasional trips to the legal card rooms around the city. It was 2000, and my marriage to my college girlfriend was midway through its collapse. We were both miserable and well aware of our misery, yet somehow the prospect of relief through divorce was still years off. To escape the tension in our cramped Noe Valley apartment, every couple of months I'd drive to Artichoke Joe's, the small, Asian-run card club about twenty minutes from our apartment.

I didn't discuss with my wife the stakes that I was playing for, and I never considered telling her of the losses that I might reasonably expect to incur. My wife didn't think much of my new hobby. My salary as an editor for a technology news site wasn't high enough so that I could reasonably choose gambling as an outlet. On those nights when I told her that I was headed for Artichoke Joe's, I got a disapproving glare in response.

Really, my silence on these matters had more to do with ignorance than any desire to deceive. My first outings were done without the benefit of even the most basic education. I hadn't read a book or even an article on poker concepts or strategies. I had no idea what I was doing. I played garbage hole cards and was oblivious to the math. But while I played, I was engrossed. Each action, each situation, was so entirely unique that it took my full concentration to determine what play was likely best. My conclusions were usually wrong, but it didn't matter. Poker provided a welcome respite from my otherwise stress-filled life.

During those outings I played the smallest game Artichoke Joe's offered, a $3–$6 fixed-limit game. In a fixed-limit game (also known, simply, as a limit game), the sizes of bets and raises in each round are predetermined. In $3–$6, for example, the first two rounds of betting require $3 bets and raises, and the second two, $6 bets and raises. I won modest amounts my first couple of sessions. Then, in my third time out, I lost $200 in four hours. I was horrified. I didn't know a loss like this was possible when dealing with such small increments. If I had done any reading at all, I would have known that even the best players could expect a $1,200 downswing in this game. Without any sort of bankroll to work out of, the $200 loss required an awkward and humiliating explanation. It marked the end of my early poker exploits.

Not until my divorce did I return to poker. Days after our separation, I hosted a game for friends in my half-furnished apartment. Then I started reading, learning about bankroll requirements and hand selection and math. After devouring my first few books, I sought local games. I figured that in a city as large as New York there must have been games, even though poker and all other kinds of gambling were illegal in the city. It only took a couple of Google searches before I found a discussion-board post from a backgammon club that was starting up some low-limit hold 'em games. I e-mailed and was offered an invitation.

It was during my initial trips to the backgammon club that I met my first poker friends—Steve, Greg, Derek, Alex, Josh, and Eric—who were, save Derek, in the early stages of their poker education. Through this new social network I was introduced to other games around the city—Greg's Friday night pot-limit game, a downtown club that had active tables every day of the week.

Soon I was playing regularly, and my bankroll began to grow. I did well in Greg's 50¢-$1 pot-limit game and was beating the $4-$8 game in the downtown club. The $200 setbacks that had so dismayed me and my ex became commonplace, occurring at least once a week, but with over $2,500 dedicated solely to poker, these losses caused no pain.

After a few months of determined play, I took some of my winnings from New York on a business trip to California and Artichoke Joe's, where I played $6-$12 limit. I had a great run there and was able to jump quickly to $10-$20 limit. One night early in my $10-$20 play, I won $1,000 and felt giddy. A couple of days later I lost $700 and was crushed. I returned to New York and played $10-$20 regularly in the downtown club until my bankroll had eclipsed $8,000.

It was about this time that I moved almost exclusively to no-limit and pot-limit hold 'em. For my first few months at these games, my conception of my bankroll didn't change much. The money was there so that I could handle the periodic spates of lousy luck—when my Aces got cracked, when I ran into set under set. In no-limit, where money could disappear so quickly, it was comforting to know that my bankroll kept me in the game.

In time I came to see that in no-limit, my bankroll could be more than a shield. That pool of money, if used correctly, could be a weapon. In a no-limit game, there was always the question of comfort, of my willingness to lose everything I put on the table. For example, just a few months into my no-limit play, I decided to take a shot at a fairly big pot-limit game that was played at New York's downtown club. I bought in for $800, while most stacks were well over $1,500, some as high as a few thousand. For the next few hours the aggressive players at the table continually put me to tough decisions, raising me off of pots, where I might well have had the best hand. Because I didn't have the proper bankroll for that game—because I was scared to lose the money in front of me—I was weak, and all but destined to finish my night with a loss.

As my bankroll has grown, I've come to feel that greater losses are completely acceptable. When I'm fully comfortable with a certain buy-in, I can take the role of aggressor and do my best to push around the weak players around me, the ones whose bankrolls don't fully equip them for the level of play in which they are engaging.

Though my trip to Foxwoods was initially jarring, I left knowing that I could rebound from some tough losses when the buy-ins were in the range of $1,000. I recovered after my first brutal day of play and proceeded to play with a freedom that showed I was willing to use my chips as weaponry when I sensed weakness. That was welcome news.

As I drove to Philadelphia, I had the happy awareness that the game I had lined up had a maximum buy-in of $500. When I finally reached the table, I thought I might be something of a menace.

I rented a Dodge Stratus for the trip, a powerful if slightly awkward sport-luxury model, because, like most New Yorkers, I didn't own a car. I'd stuffed about half my wardrobe into the backseat and ample trunk, figuring I needed to be prepared for both the harsh winter weather I was encountering in the Northeast and warm days I'd likely see in Texas and southern California. I also brought my laptop, my favorite pillow, my iPod, and a set of poker chips, should I need to play host to an impromptu game.

The drive from Foxwoods to Philadelphia was trying. Hours of rain over I-95 and the New Jersey Turnpike, both packed and fast-moving, left me exhausted. Over one particularly harrowing stretch of the turnpike, with hurtling cars within what seemed mere inches on either side, I was happy that I paid extra for the sturdier midsize car, which held well to the wet road.

This long drive provided the first opportunity I'd had to marvel at my situation. The money to pay for the car, hotels, and everything else on the trip would come from a pool provided by my publisher. In a way, I thought I'd achieved one of the great hustles in the history of gambling. Essentially, through my representatives, I'd said to a variety of publishers, "I'm going to travel and play poker for three months. I'll likely win some money and meet some bizarre people along the way, and I'll write about it. How about you pay for the whole thing?" Their response: "Sure, sounds good."

I decided to approach the trip with an open schedule. I didn't want to tie myself into any specific location for any period of time. That would allow me to point my car in the direction of any interesting game that I happened to hear about. It would give me some needed flexibility when weather was sure to impact my priorities. For the entirety of the trip, I had only two preplanned stops. In January, I'd spend time in Tunica, Mississippi, so that I'd hit the action around the World Poker Open at Jack Binion's casino, and I'd conclude my trip in March at the Los Angeles Poker Classic, where, if things went well, I'd be able to play in the high-stakes games.

The remainder of the schedule was open. I'd head south, in hopes of avoiding as much snow and cold as I could. I'd stick to urban areas, where finding games would be easier. But these constraints were self-imposed. The reality was, I was free. I could go wherever my car, my money, and my interests would take me.

After arriving in Philadelphia, I took a short nap at the hotel to prepare myself for a night of cards. From all I'd heard, Philadelphia's poker scene was similar to New York's, only smaller. Gambling was illegal there as well, but there were a number of underground clubs around the city. As long as these clubs were discreet and shied away from games like blackjack and craps, the cops left them alone.

With the club's address copied from an e-mail exchange I'd had with the manager, I took a cab to a tony restaurant district. The office building holding the club sat between moderately busy Italian and Mexican spots. I stood outside the building whose number matched the one I had scribbled down, but I was still unsure. The building's directory gave no indication that a poker club was inside, and I had no idea which of the buttons above the directory would ring the club. Before pressing random buttons, the door buzzed: Someone had released the lock and allowed me entry. The club must have had a security camera watching the door and someone inside caught sight of me and decided I wasn't a cop. Once inside, I was still without a destination. I walked from door to door until I heard the clicking of chips.

I entered a space that was brightly lit and slightly claustrophobic. The four oval poker tables consumed nearly all the room's space. The tables' felts were threadbare, and the sloppily framed wall decorations—dogs playing poker, a *Rounders* poster—decorated the scarred walls. Near the entryway, steam rose from a few Sterno-heated covered stainless steel serving dishes.

Two of the tables were active. At the table farthest from the door, a very competitive-looking game of 7-stud was under way. There was probably $10,000 on the table in front of a few men in their fifties and sixties. It seemed they were playing $75-$150 limit, which was way too big a game for me.

At the front table, considerably younger men—ranging from twenty-two to forty—had far smaller stacks in front of them. This, I was told, was the $2-$5 no-limit game, and the max buy-in was $500.

I peeled off that sum and sat. It was a friendly group. There was more good-natured conversation in the first hour than I'd heard in my three days at Foxwoods. A few of the players, I learned, belonged to some sort of fraternal organization, and they griped about the management of one of the club's activities. A softball team, I thought, as it seemed to fit with their age and gruff blue-collar demeanor. But that didn't make sense in the very bureaucratic context they were describing, so I inquired. They said that their organization annually staged something akin to a Broadway musical. I thought they were kidding, and I nearly chuckled. I couldn't see these guys putting on, say, *Thoroughly Modern Millie*. But I stopped myself, and I was glad. This was clearly no laughing matter. "Artistic differences?" I asked. I received only a vague shrug in reply.

I expected this table to be tougher than the ones at Foxwoods. There was no tourist element here—no craps player just itching to blow off five grand. Underground clubs like this generally draw a more determined sort of player, guys whose love or addiction compels them to play. That was fine with me. Playing against crazy, unschooled gamblers who find their way to casinos is profitable but uninteresting. Against someone who's willing to play any two cards for any amount of money, there's really only one effective strategy: Wait for a hand. Such a player can't be bluffed; he'll call with anything. Accurate reads are pretty much impossible against someone whose actions are unreasoned. All I can do is pray for quality cards and try not to fall asleep.

The competition in this club offered more opportunities. These guys had some decent knowledge: They knew how to value a hand, and they were familiar with the language of bets and raises. But I also got the sense that the $500 buy-in was as much as these guys wanted to play for—it was the top of their comfort range. This was great for me, as they might be playing a little scared. After Foxwoods, the $500 didn't feel like a whole lot. Hell, I'd lost five times that in three hours.

After an hour of fairly tight play, I was in middle position and there was a limper to me. I raised to $25 with 7♥-8♦. This is a trash hand in no-limit, and I'm well aware of that, but the table was a bit tight—players were cautious, unwilling to commit chips—and I was trying to generate some action.

All folded to the limper, who called. The flop was 7♣-3♣-3♦.

The limper checked to me, and I bet $40. He quickly check-raised to $140. (See Fig. 3.)

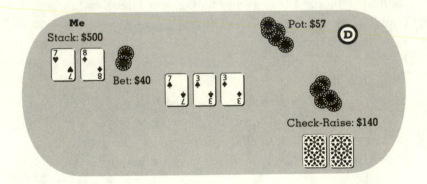

I didn't act immediately. I stopped and thought. Could he have pocket 7s, for a full house, 7s full of 3s? Unlikely. Most players will slow-play a hand that big, feign weakness with the hope the opponent will be lured into betting on the turn or the river. A lone 3, for trip 3s? I doubted it. That would be a similar candidate for slow-playing.

In the end only one hand made sense to me: a flush draw. Many people will raise aggressively on a draw with the logic that they have two ways of winning. They can win if their opponent folds or if they hit their draw. It's known as a semi-bluff. I figured he had something like A♣-9♣.

If that was true, I had the best hand and had only one recourse. "Another $300," I announced.

He quickly tossed his hand in the muck. Curious to know if my deduction was correct, I showed my cards and asked if I had the best hand. He slumped in his chair. No, he told me, my hand wasn't the best. He had pocket 9s and figured with the way I was betting that I had pocket Kings or Aces.

After showing this piece of crap and winning on what the rest of the table thought was a bluff, I had no credibility. In my opponents' eyes I was absolutely willing to commit my entire stack on damn close to nothing. Therefore, they reasoned, I'd need to be called down when I tried to bully my way to a pot.

About twenty minutes later I was in the small blind with pocket 4s. There were two limpers to me, and I matched the big blind. Four of us saw a flop of 3♣-3♦-4♦. (See Fig. 4.)

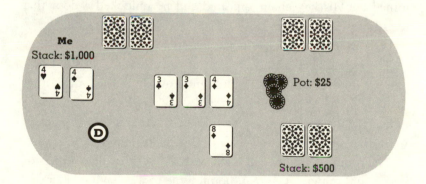

I flopped a full house, 4s full of 3s. A monster. Usually this is a hand that can be slow-played. I'd want an opponent to bet for me, or maybe hit a card on the turn or river that would give him the false hope that he could take the pot, but my situation was somewhat different—I had no credibility. As far as the table was concerned, I'd bet with anything. In fact, leading at this pot—betting at it from the start—might do a whole lot more to disguise the strength of my hand than checking, then calling a bet. So I bet out $15. I got a call from middle position, and then the same guy I'd bluffed off of 9s earlier raised to $45. Poor schmuck. I smooth-called. The middle-position player also called.

The turn was the J♥.

I checked. Middle position checked and my unfortunate friend bet $60. I raised to $125. Middle position folded, and my late-position buddy called.

The river was truly gorgeous: Q♦.

If he was on a flush draw, he made his hand, and there was almost no way he could fold. I bet $300, and he quickly raised his remaining $150. I called, and he turned over his A♦-J♦.

A couple of hours later, I opted to cash out with my $1,200 profit. I informed the manager, a heavyset young Asian man, who told me to rack my chips and walk toward the back of the club. As I did, a rail-thin gray-haired man from the stud game got up and joined us. His key chain appeared and he unlocked a door that seemed to lead to a closet.

"Go on in," he said, gesturing for me to lead the way.

The man looked kindly enough, and a little frail, but still I hesitated. I'd never been to this club, and nobody in the world other than the present company knew exactly where I was. In my entire poker-playing life, I'd never been asked to enter a closetlike space with strangers, but I didn't see any choice, so I entered.

The room was small and lined with shelves that held a mess of papers and folders. The man pointed me to a decaying chair. He sat in a rickety office chair at a small desk while the Asian kid stood beside me. As far as I could tell, he didn't have access to any weaponry.

"So what the hell did you do to that game?" the man asked.

"Sorry. What?"

"Arnold told me that you tore those guys up. You a pro or something?"

"I got great cards."

"Oh, come on." It was then I noticed his appreciative smile. "You don't need cards to beat those guys." He slapped me on the leg and laughed.

I told him about the book and my poker credentials. He seemed impressed. He then told me about his own career. He was a longtime pro who played high-stakes stud along the East Coast. He'd made money playing poker when the games were brutally tough, in a bygone day when the waters weren't full of fish. He'd sat down at tables full of pros in Atlantic City, because it was the only game around.

"Things have really changed," he concluded.

"For the better," I added. If we had been drinking, we would have toasted the brilliant days our game was enjoying.

He told me his name was Don, and through some conversation, I got the feeling that, although things had gotten much better for skilled players, he was nostalgic for the days of ten and twenty years ago, when the organized East Coast poker world was populated by a few hundred degenerates.

"I'd walk into the Taj, and I knew everybody. It was like family," he said. "But not anymore."

It was late, and I didn't feel comfortable asking about what he'd given up to be part of the games in Atlantic City. If he found his surrogate family in a casino's poker room, how could he possibly have maintained a real family of his own? I wondered if his nostalgia was mixed with a healthy heaping of regret.


In poker terms, I owned the Philadelphia game. But the control was only possible because I felt free to use my chips as weapons. When I incorrectly decided that my pair of 7s was best, it was my aggression that bought me the pot—my willingness to act as though I had Aces. And I was only willing to do this because I had a bankroll that was far in excess of what I needed for the game I was playing. I was entirely comfortable losing everything in front of me. Later, my seeming indifference to money provoked some bad calls when I had great cards.

At the other end of this trip, after I'd finally reached Los Angeles, I'd be playing in a game where I could reasonably expect to have ten times as much money on the table as I had in Philadelphia. During the intervening three months, I had to do my best to acquire the money that would allow me to play with a similar freedom at the elevated stakes.

Even if I managed to pad my bankroll sufficiently and win the $20,000 I set as my goal, I had questions about my fortitude, my willingness to bet $3,000 with the same casual air I could put out $300. The idea of losing that much in a single hand or four times that over a few rotten days was daunting. The sums seemed impossibly large, and I didn't know if I was capable of enduring that kind of beating.

The fact that I had to engage in this sort of introspection was evidence of a disposition that can be highly problematic for a poker player. The top pros, the best in the world, seem to share some recessive trait that allows them to view money as an inconsequential commodity. Stories circulate through the poker world of top pros who have won hundreds of thousands at poker games, only to lose it all at the craps tables. Many pros, of course, manage to play for vertiginously high stakes while maintaining fiscal discipline away from the table. But most of the best players do well because they have little concern for the value of the chips they are playing with. They make the best plays because they're the best plays. If they were to stop and think, "My God, I could either bluff here or buy a Jaguar with that money," discretion would rule the play. As my actions in Philadelphia proved, caution and discretion are not traits that correlate well with high-quality poker.

As I considered my goals and assessed my current abilities, I understood that for me there would be a limit, a level at which I would say, *I simply can't play this high. The stakes are too much for me.* But I hadn't hit that limit yet, and I needed to reach higher if I was going to make the kind of money I needed to support a family. I could do that with the Commerce game, and if I managed to gather the necessary bankroll during the rest of the trip, I was hopeful that I'd be able to manage the inflows and outflows of cash.

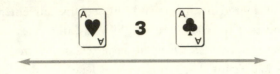

# ATLANTIC CITY

In the years before World War II, Atlantic City was a favored destination for well-off families all over the East. Trains from New York and Philadelphia brought in vacationers eager for sea air, exhilarating rides, and first-class nightlife. In the thirties and forties, the top big bands and best crooners, including Sinatra, played the city regularly. But the growth of air travel after the war made Florida, the West Coast, and Europe more appealing destinations for the upper crust, and Atlantic City couldn't compete. By the seventies, Atlantic City was a shell of its former self. Crime was rampant, unemployment was high, and drugs were everywhere.

In 1976, New Jerseyians passed a ballot initiative, known as the Casino Control Act, which legalized gambling in Atlantic City. The campaign was hard-fought and closely decided. The majority of state voters concluded that gambling was a vice somewhat preferable to heroin. If all went well, the gaming income would, as the Casino Control Act put it, "facilitate the redevelopment of existing blighted areas."

Casinos operators were thrilled with the opportunity to bring Vegas-style destinations to a spot only two hours from New York

City, an hour from Philadelphia, and a few hours from Washington, D.C. In 1978, Resorts International opened the first casino in Atlantic City. Resorts and the casinos that followed did reasonably well. But the Casino Control Act restricted gaming licenses, granting them only to full-service resort-casino-hotel operators. To open a gaming room, a company's plans had to include a hotel, restaurants, bars, and nightclubs. The perverse outcome of this limitation was that tourists never had a reason to leave their hotel casino. Why venture to restaurants or shops on surrounding streets when everything was so close at hand?

So, despite the windfalls that casinos accumulated, surrounding businesses saw essentially no positive impact. Casino employees did all right, but many moved to the suburbs and the city itself languished. For years—decades, actually—Atlantic City had the deserved reputation of being a dangerous, drug-infested ghetto that happened to have casinos. Visitors knew that, upon arrival, they should check into their casino hotels and stay within their protected confines until checkout.

Things have improved somewhat in recent years. State authorities made a concerted effort to clean out the drug dens and stem the crime. The progress was noticeable when I arrived. The Super 8 Motel I stayed in—the $79 Internet special was irresistible—was in a part of the city that could no longer be classified as blighted. Just a few blocks from the the Taj Mahal, Resorts International, and the Boardwalk, this area was once dotted with syringe-strewn empty lots. Now the lots are just empty—and that's an improvement.

I pulled into the Super 8's parking lot, and did a quick survey of the area. Across the street next to the well-swept lot, there was both a bar and a halfway house. A rail-thin threesome exited the halfway house and ambled out of sight. Then several teens wearing oversized basketball jerseys, do-rags, and baggy jeans walked down the street and stopped at the entrance of the parking lot. I did a quick mental inventory of my possessions in the car. I had more than $6,000 in cash in my front pocket and a laptop full of invaluable and not-recently-backed-up information. I tensed and made no effort to gather my items or move toward check-in.

My anxiety was ridiculous. The teens were simply enjoying their after-school freedom. They weren't doing anything unsavory or threatening, and I'm not the kind of person who thinks ungenerously about groups, even those whose demographics correlate closely with high crime. I am progressive—a reasonably educated and nonjudgmental Northeasterner. I speak liberal fluently. I read *The New York Times* and listen to NPR. I live in a Brooklyn neighborhood that's equal parts black and white, and I feel absolutely comfortable there, even after the robbery.

All of this notwithstanding, I couldn't find my way out of the car and past the group to the Super 8's check-in. I restarted the car with the intention of heading directly to the Taj Mahal, where I'd get a safe-deposit box before checking in. I'd feel some guilt for my actions, I realized, but at the moment I didn't much care.

After three hours of play at the Taj, I was starting to hate the man directly across the table from me. He was younger than me, probably twenty-nine, with a broad build, solid jaw, and tight, wavy brown hair. He dressed well, with a casual patrician elegance that seemed neither overreaching nor pretentious. His girlfriend provided the perfect accessory. She came by the table a couple of times in the afternoon, and necks invariably craned at nearby tables. Blond and fit and shapely and tall, wearing a designer form-fitted T-shirt and a short skirt, each time she appeared, she held a couple of additional shopping bags from expensive stores. He was spending the day playing poker—and absolutely destroying the table—while providing this stunning creature with the means to enjoy her day. She would come by, and he'd pull out his money clip and casually hand her some bills so that she could keep herself occupied in the stores.

Though I didn't want to admit it, streaks of envy developed within me as I watched him. I don't know if there's a guy alive— from the darkest nihilistic poet to the most pious born-again— who doesn't occasionally fantasize about the joys of an existence like the one I was witnessing. Who wouldn't want to be flush with cash and clad in couture while entertaining a woman with a spectacular body you'd assuredly enjoy thoroughly and repeatedly?

But what was particularly galling about this man was the way he was playing poker. He wasn't especially skilled or knowledgeable, of that I was certain. But on this afternoon, he was the beneficiary of a terrific run of cards. As fortune turned his way, his confidence rose, and before long he'd managed to put the rest of the table on the defensive. He was aggressive, playing what must have been the best poker of his life, making a couple of great calls and picking the perfect moments to bluff.

By contrast, my day had been filled with a series of annoyances. It took me a half hour of testy discussions with managers before I got my safe-deposit box. Then I had to wait nearly an hour to get into a game. In my first big pot of the afternoon, which was played against Mr. Perfect, I found myself screaming at as much of the Taj staff as I could get to listen.

In the hand, I had raised in late position with Q♦-J♦. Mr. Perfect called from the big blind. The flop was 9♠-T♥-4♦—I had an open-ended straight draw. It was checked to me, and I bet the pot, which was $50. Mr. Perfect announced a raise. He then moved a stack of reds, $100, in front of his cards. He then came back to his stacks two more times, to gather $250 more dollars, making the total bet $350.

"That's a string bet," I said to the dealer. The rule in poker is pretty straightforward: A player can make only one forward motion toward the pot. If the player has announced the exact size of the bet, he can take as many trips back and forth as he likes. But in a case like this, when a player says simply "raise" and then moves a specific amount of chips forward, he cannot go back to his stack. The rule is designed so that players don't continually shuttle chips back and forth in order to elicit some reaction. In this instance, I needed to have the rule enforced. With only a $50 raise, I had the chance to call and hit my straight and maybe double up. But with his full raise I had no choice but to fold.

"No. No string," said the dealer, who seemed unfamiliar with English articles. "He say raise. He can go back to stack."

I explained what I knew the rule to be.

"No."

"Call the floor," I demanded.

A floor manager came over. The situation was explained, and an improper ruling, one echoing the dealer's interpretation, was given.

"Why don't you get a rule book," I suggested. "You don't know what you're talking about."

He thought. "We can check the book. But that's my ruling on this hand. Now you have to act."

Digusted, I folded. About five minutes later the floor man returned. He told me that he had checked the book, and indeed I was right. That was a string bet.

"It might be a good idea if the staff actually knew the rules of the game," I barked.

He walked away and Mr. Perfect chimed in, "Guess I got really lucky on that one." He was trying to be gracious. So on top of being rich, handsome, and fucking lucky, he was decent and friendly. His girlfriend had settled down in a chair beside him, and her smooth, tanned legs and perky breasts were somehow goading me.

A couple of more raises were met with reraises, to which I folded. I later had no choice but to lay down a top two-pair when an obvious flush hit the board. It was then that I became hyperaware of the P.A. system just outside the poker room. In a continuous loop it was blaring about the "Survive the Boardroom" game. Apparently it had some tie-in to Trump's reality TV series, *The Apprentice*. The specifics of the rules eluded me, but my ears couldn't seem to escape two phrases that were repeated once every minute. The first was a clip of the Donald saying, "You're fired." The second was the game's motto, spoken by a dulcet female voice: "Survive the boardroom. It's not just a game, it's an experience." Over the course of a few hours, the senselessness of the phrase got under my skin. What the hell could that phrase mean? The people who worked here knew the English language about as well as they knew the rules of poker.

As annoyance and impatience welled within me, I found King-Queen in late position—one to the right of the button—and raised. The big blind then reraised. Yet another goddamn reraise, I thought. I was sick of it. I decided that I'd taken enough; I was no pushover. At that moment I thought King-Queen, a hand which I normally treat with the caution one affords a rabid raccoon, was worth all of my chips. I came over the top all-in. The blind quickly called and showed pocket Kings. Another $450 gone.

I was on tilt.


The word "tilt" was co-opted from pinball. A tilted machine shuts down after a player rocks or smacks it excessively. In poker, a tilted player, reacting to the brutality of the deck or his surroundings, acts as I did at the Taj—blasting off chips, berating other players, or otherwise playing or behaving badly. Tilt is a specific form of temporary insanity. Thankfully, most tilt-inspired infractions are entirely self-injurious and are therefore nonprosecutable. And that's a good thing, because tilt is frightfully common. So common, in fact, that when my peers and I review the losses of a particularly nasty session, we will always ask of one another, "How much of that was tilt?"

Once I chatted with Howard "the Professor" Lederer, one of the top players in the world, about tilt. He said a tilting player plays badly because on some level he's determined that playing well is irrelevant. He'll lose anyway, the perverted logic goes, so why not hunt for some ridiculous draws or make some nonsensical raises. Howard has studied eastern religion, and is almost disturbingly calm at the table. In all situations, he seems attentive but unfazed—a long, long way from tilt. Was tilt ever a problem for Howard, the calmest man in poker? He said that for the first fifteen years or so of his poker career tilt was an issue, but he's since learned to calmly endure the vagaries of the game. He recommends *Zen in the Art of Archery,* and *The Tao of Poker* for those looking to improve their games.

So in a mere twelve years I might be completely tilt-free. That is, if I take up Buddhism.

In almost every session I've ever played, there's been one player who curses the deck, his opponent's stupidity, or the innate unfairness of the game. When a player seems on the verge of losing his mind, the good players around him take on vulturous looks. It's at that moment when he's most likely to do something stupid, maybe attempt an audacious bluff or make a ridiculous call.

Like most, I simply react to my tilting opposition. I might make a call I wouldn't otherwise consider or forgo a bluff at a time when my adversary is in no mood to fold. Still, I don't go into a poker game looking to cause tilt. A group of Stanford grads who took up poker in the midnineties did just that: They went into their games with the express purpose of tilting those around them and each other. They called themselves, aptly enough, the Tiltboys. They traveled to Vegas several times and wrote hilarious trip reports that they posted at www.tiltboys.com and later turned into the book *Tales From the Tiltboys.* A small excerpt from one of the trip reports (with minor edits) reads:

> I [Perry] just beat this older guy who was already hemorrhaging money and tilting by showing him AA on the river. Pot was capped preflop, so he probably had KK or QQ.

*The guy agonized over the decision to call the river, and after he called and saw my cards, he nodded moodily and disgustedly flung his cards. Then he hung his head and stared at his diminishing stack.*

*Rafe, in a bright, whipper-snapper tone of voice: "You had Queens didn't you? I'll bet that's what you had." The guy slowly looked up at Rafe and said nothing. Rafe: "Queens? Did you have Queens? Queens. That's a bummer."*

*I was feeling sorry for the guy, and thinking Rafe didn't realize how absolutely annoying his pestering must have been to this guy, so I whispered: "Rafe, that's bad poker etiquette. Don't ask somebody what they had after they folded."*

*Then I joked: "Of course, if you're trying to get him on tilt, that's another story."*

*Rafe, fully serious: "I know it's bad etiquette. I am trying to get him on tilt."*

Along with verbal punishment, the Tiltboys used their actions to induce tilt. The Rafe referred to in the post is Rafe Furst. I have occasionally played against him. Rafe would enter a table and start raising, or if he wasn't raising, he was reraising. He'd get caught raising with crap and lose some pots, but it didn't matter, he continued raising. At first he'd lose. Usually he'd burn through two full buy-ins.

His constant, seemingly mindless aggression would eventually lead to a group psychosis. Nobody at the table could accept that Rafe ever connected with a flop or started with a big hand. When he did catch, he inevitably got paid off. Before long the action at the table was riotous. The most sedate players would end up committing huge portions of their stacks regularly, even when Rafe wasn't involved in the pot. The griping that was originally targeted at Rafe spread through the table. Eventually Rafe would be ahead—way ahead—and the people around him would be left scratching their chins wondering how this lucky bastard accumulated so much money. Even after Rafe tightened up, they'd whine and bitch and call him down with horrible hands. Per his plan, the entire table was on tilt.

I think the Tiltboys' tactics can be viewed as extraordinarily vicious. Chip Reese or Doyle Brunson will happily and speedily take all their opponent's money, but I've never heard that either had any interest in driving his opponents crazy. At some level the Tiltboys' verbal needling and other tilt-inspiring antics seem cruel or even misanthropic.

I've gotten to know Rafe, and I've found him to be nothing but generous and charming and funny. He makes friends easily, and seems to remember everyone he's talked with. When I started the trip, Rafe offered a list of friends from across the country I could call to inquire about games. In every case, the person I contacted was happy to hear from someone who knew Rafe. People are drawn to him. They remember the interest he showed in their stories and lives.

If there's a contradiction between his at-the-table brutality and his overall kindness, Rafe doesn't see it. In an e-mail, he said, "Given that a poker table is a competitive arena wherein people choose to sit and interact with each other, I think that what goes on at the table socially is akin to what happens at the bottom of a rugby scrum or underneath the surface of the water in water polo. There are rules of conduct, and if you violate those rules, you should be punished. But a certain amount of antagonism goes along with competition, and luckily you get to choose who you compete against at any given time by choosing your table (unlike most organized sports).

"Outside the ring, so to speak, there's no contradiction in being a kind, courteous person."

I think Rafe's use of rugby and boxing metaphors reveals an aspect of poker that most players fail to acknowledge. I'll stick with the boxing comparison to make the point. When a young talent is brought on the scene, his promoters seek opponents who offer no real challenge or threat. The goal is to build an impressive win-loss record and show evidence of knockout power.

The gifted boxer must have the willingness to inflict potentially deadly blows on a man who he knows is all but defenseless and whose award for the beating may be no more than a couple of hundred dollars. The talented boxer may be a good man to family and friends, but that doesn't make his in-the-ring actions any less brutal or cruel. To make it in boxing, he must have some capacity for brutality and cruelty. Without it, success is impossible.

I believe the same can be said for poker players. Rafe or I or anyone else who succeeds at this game must have the willingness to cause damage. If we take some joy in wreaking havoc, all the better. The Tiltboys celebrated the lunacy they caused on a Web site and now in a book. While I'm not as public in my revelry, I relish the high I get after dismantling an opponent. Knowing that I've manipulated a man into surrendering something he holds dear brings about a malevolent pride that is wonderfully addictive.

I imagine that after I blasted off my chips at the Taj, my opponents took some relish in the tilt they had wrought.


A fiancée should have to endure a lot, I think. When someone accepts the idea of a lifetime of shared experience, he or she should be willing to find interest in what would otherwise seem like pointless minutiae. I'm no Dr. Phil, but I'm pretty sure this is right. I do acknowledge, however, that no future wife or husband should be forced to talk his or her beloved off of tilt.

"Oh, sweetie," Marisa said when I called to tell her about the Taj fiasco. "Didn't you say that everyone tilts?"

"Yeah," I replied, so grateful that she remembered these things.

I looked around my hotel room. The bed was noticeably bowed in the middle and the bedspread was threadbare. A two-by-four sat in the rail of the sliding window, ensuring that the only means of entry was by bashing through the glass.

"You know," I went on, "I'm only two hours away. Maybe I'll come home."

"Oh. That would be great."

"But I just started the trip. I—"

"I know, you really shouldn't."

"Tell me about your night, sweetie," I said. And for the next fifteen minutes she told me about seeing our friend Liz perform in an off-Broadway play. It was a postmodern staging, and getting any sense of it required long and strange descriptions. As best as I could tell, Liz played a male dressed as a woman who stood silent on the stage, occasionally offering a few words or a short tune from her violin. As I tried to visualize the setting, the remnants of tilt within me melted away.

When we finished with that topic, Marisa piped in, "You've been playing for over a week straight. Maybe it's time for a day off."

I agreed. I needed a day for some post-tilt reflection. If I could find a way to more or less control myself after a $1,700 robbery, I should be able to calm my nerves after an error that cost me a third as much.

As I settled into bed and flipped through the dismal offerings from cable TV, I thought about Marisa. In our three years together she has been unfailingly kind and generous—never cruel, never mean, never greedy.

For three years she commuted an hour and a half each way to the South Bronx, where she taught at one of the most disadvantaged schools in one of the city's most dysfunctional neighborhoods. And she never complained. She never revealed even the slightest bit of bigotry. That night I felt she was a better person than I was. And a lot more than I deserved.

I moved from the Super 8 to Atlantic City's newest and best hotel, the Borgata. It is beautiful, tastefully designed, with large, comfortable rooms. Its poker room is smaller than the Taj's, but the tables are new, the chips are clean, the dealers are competent, and the pools of fish are well stocked.

In my first session I found myself sitting next to a thin man in his fifties with a slight Greek accent who talked incessantly, but had only one topic: his crappy luck.

"Look at that," he'd say as a flop of 9-9-2 hit the board. "I had a 9 last hand. This time, all 9s. Harumph."

"Can you believe this, I have a pair of 8s and lose. Jeeze."

An hour into this game, I was in a tough spot. I was holding A♥-Q♥ and the board was A♦-Q♣-J♦-T♦. I had top two-pair but was facing a large bet on the turn, where the T♦ made a straight or flush a real possibility. I hadn't held a hand as big as two-pair in hours, but any hand with a King would have crushed me. The bet came from an opponent who was new to the table, and I didn't know if he was capable of bluffing in such a situation.

The Greek turned to me. "Can you believe this? With the last hand, I'd have a royal flush. Unbelievable. I don't know how—"

"Would you shut up!" For the first time on the trip, I'd screamed at another player.

I would have wondered if I was out of line had the dealer not chimed in, "Let the guy make his decision."

I folded and left that session with a loss.

But I had two more days at the Borgata, and those went well. Some fish had migrated into the poker room just as I caught some cards. The play wasn't particularly interesting, but I was pleased with two consecutive wins. I managed to leave Atlantic City with a profit.

After a week of near-continuous play, I was up about $1,500.

# VIRGINIA

**T**HIS ROAD TRIP WAS NOT MY FIRST POKER–RELATED travel. With my New York friends I'd made several journeys, a few to Foxwoods, a couple to Atlantic City, one to Los Angeles, and a couple to Vegas. The trips always corresponded with major tournaments, and we were just a few of the thousands of players who descended upon a spot hoping to summon enough skill and luck to score big in a tournament. But even if the tournaments went poorly, there was still ample reason to take such an outing. The big tournaments attracted so many players that there was always a good game to draw our interest.

In the previous sentence, the adjective "good" has a very specific meaning, one known to poker pros everywhere. It means the games were easily beatable. It means there were at least a couple of fish in the waters. It means the players sucked. Even with plenty of good games to choose from, the excursions didn't always go well. On one Foxwoods trip, each of the four of us who went ended the stay badly stuck and miserable. The L.A. jaunt proved disastrous for one friend and his backers as he attempted to move to higher limits. But no matter the outcome, the purpose—to find the good games, to seek out the fish—was perfectly sensible.

For me, these excursions provided some unexpected highlights, for it was in these tournaments and the cash games that surrounded them that I got my first experience playing against some of the game's most prominent players, pros recognizable to everyone who plays serious poker. My first confrontation against a known pro came in L.A., where I played a panicky and incoherent hand against Ron Rose. In Atlantic City, Allen Cunningham effortlessly took half my stack. But over time, I settled into such confrontations. At Foxwoods, I bluffed Chris Moneymaker off a moderate pot and showed him my second-best hand. In Vegas, after a couple of memorable encounters against Erik Seidel, he asked me, "Are you a pro?" I was walking on air.

These encounters seemed to be occurring frequently. Soon I'd played notable hands against Layne Flack, Paul Darden, Erick Lindgren, and Howard Lederer. After several of these bouts, it didn't take a whole lot of introspection to conclude that at some level I was seeking out these confrontations. I had made the trip because of the good games, because of the hunting grounds full of cash-laden fish. But when the opportunities arose, I sought to pit myself against the best.

This pattern continued in the most startling way when I traveled to Aruba. I was playing in the $6,000 buy-in Aruba Classic. I'd won a $200 online tournament, a "satellite," that secured my entry. After a few hours of play, Mike "the Mouth" Matusow was moved to my table. Mike is a portly man with Semitic features and thick, curly black hair. His nickname is well earned. At unpredictable moments, Mike will shout remarks that are at best inappropriate and at worst offensive. During one memorable and televised encounter at the main event of the 2004 World Series, Mike bluffed the eventual winner, Greg Raymer, out of a pot. Mike showed his cards, then screamed, "I got big balls. . . . You got *tiny* balls."

Mike is one of a very few poker players who has gained the

enmity of his peers. "I just don't like him," I overheard a top pro saying after one of his outbursts. Late in the Aruba tournament, Antonio "the Magician" Esfandiari, a young pro with a sharp tongue, got so sick of Matusow's continual blatherings that he made a unique offer. "What's it worth to get you not to talk to me for three months?" Esfandiari asked. "It's got to be worth $30,000."

Matusow looked genuinely hurt.

The hand I played against Matusow came in the first day of the Aruba event. After a few hours of action, I was doing well. My cards were running hot and I was getting good value when I hit a hand. We started with stacks of $12,000 and I'd managed to build mine to over $25,000. But the table had gotten tough. In addition to Matusow, Marcel Luske, an outstanding Dutch player and affable mouth in his own right, was moved to my immediate right.

The blinds were $300 and $600, and each player had to post a $75 ante. I had a trash hand, Q-4, in the small blind, something I'd happily throw in the muck if the pot had been raised. But Matusow, in early position, simply called the big blind, as did Marcel Luske, who was on the button. So when the action got to me, there was $2,850 in the pot, and it cost me only $300 to call. I was getting a great price to try to hit a miracle flop; something like Q-4-4 would have been nice.

The flop wasn't a miracle: 3♦-3♣-T♦. A total miss for me. For a reason I cannot possibly explain, I instantly decided to play the hand as though I had a 3. To an extent this made tactical sense. It would be very unlikely that either Matusow or Luske would voluntarily put money into the pot with a hand that contained a 3. But me, I was a blind. Given the odds I was getting to make the call preflop, I could have just about anything. Matusow and Luske would clearly be aware of this.

How would I play trip 3s? I'd likely slow-play. So I checked. Matusow bet out $2,000—a strong bet, sort of saying to the field that he had a 10, for top pair, and would be happy if everyone

folded. Luske folded, and I smooth-called. Figure 5 shows what
the table looked like at the completion of the flop betting.

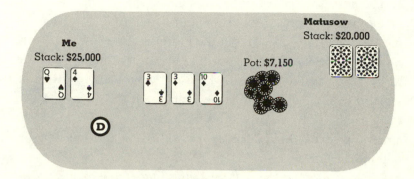

The turn brought the A♦. I checked again. Matusow hesitated.
He was trying to figure out whether I had the diamond flush
draw or the made hand. He decided I was on the draw and bet
out $5,000.

It was back to me and it was gut-check time. I had nothing—
garbage, no outs at all. And the bluff would cost me most of the
stack I'd taken hours to build. I clearly remember asking myself,
"Do you have the nerve for this?" After nearly a full minute of
hesitation I said, "Raise." I reached into my stack and tried to think
of a bet that was both large enough to get a fold but small enough
to seem as though I wanted a call. "Thirteen thousand," I said.

Matusow quickly mucked, and I managed to exhale. I tilted my
cards up, at an angle where I could admire them. Matusow, across
the table, was looking directly at the back of my cards and asked,
"Did you have the three?" I nodded and threw my cards away.
But my seat bordered an area where some spectators had gathered.
A few of the onlookers, including one of Matusow's friends,
caught sight of the cards. He told Mike what I had.

Mike complimented my play—"just got outplayed for half my
stack"—and went on to discuss the hand with a couple of other

people in the area. I was numb. The terror that should have flooded me during the hand hit me a few minutes later. For the next five minutes, my hands shook.

The next day, I ended up at the same table as Layne Flack, one of the best tournament players alive. Soon after he sat, he asked me, "Are you the guy who put the move on Mike?" I was, I told him. He gave me a gentle warning about continuing to make such plays. I couldn't figure if he was giving genuine advice or looking to forestall similar moves I might make on him. Since then, I've heard Layne discuss his table banter—how most of it is a means of extracting information or otherwise manipulating his opponents.

I managed to cash in in Aruba, finishing eightieth and taking home $8,000. Matusow finished third, for $250,000, and Flack finished second, nabbing $500,000. Clearly my burst of superior play didn't affect Matusow too badly. And why would it? He got outplayed for about two minutes. It was one hand in the course of thousands he played in that tournament, hundreds of thousands he'd play in the year. Matusow, like any good poker player, knows that one's ability can't be judged by any single hand or short series of hands. The best players—the top pros—are those who make the best choices over the course of the hundreds of thousands of decisions that the game forces a player to make.

If I were to assume that this single moment of superiority was all I needed to know about my ability compared to a player of Matusow's skills, I'd be falling into the same net that snares so many fish who have shared a table with me. These fish bluff, show their cards, become full of themselves, then bluff again. Then they get caught, lose everything, and leave broke. Somehow they manage to overlook the net loss the evening provided. They point to the fact that they outplayed me on three of four hands as proof of their skills. Then they come back with more money and the cycle repeats.

So does the hand against Matusow say anything of my worthiness to play with the best players? Not at all.

If I were going to succeed on the trip, I had to acknowledge that the seeking of such encounters was folly. Even if I managed to emerge with a profit from similar conflicts with world-class pros, such hands were too risky. I was too likely to get outplayed. And I was not in a spot where I could play for the sake of satisfying my ego or stroking my pride.

For the rest of the trip, as I attempted to assess the viability of a career in poker, I couldn't allow myself to be seduced by some notion that I might be *great*. For the sake of my bankroll, for the sake of accumulating the money I needed to play the $10–$20 at Commerce, I needed to put such ideas aside. I had to focus on the fish. And as I was heading into the South, where hunting was said to be a popular pastime, I was hopeful that my pursuit would reap bountiful results.

To get to the Fair Stream Poker Club, about thirty miles south of Washington, D.C., I exited I-95, drove past a Western Warehouse and a gun store to an industrial park. Amid the auto body shops, the light industrial facilities, and the warehouses stood an unmarked door with a security camera eyeing the entrance. Even south of the Mason-Dixon Line, I could spot a poker club from a considerable distance.

I found the club through a Web site that lists various home games. I had exchanged e-mails and talked on the phone with Dave, one of the club's proprietors, before arriving. I told him about the book and the magazines I'd written for. Poker was illegal in Virginia, and I wanted to quell any fears Dave might have of letting a stranger through the door.

I entered into a small anteroom with a large desk, behind which sat a burly middle-aged man. I introduced myself and received a warm greeting. This was Dave.

"Seems you're OK," he said after a handshake. "I made some calls."

"Yeah? Who did you talk to?" I wondered if we had some common acquaintances in the New York poker world.

Dave would not reveal his sources. I dropped names of some club owners around the tristate area in an effort to provoke conversation, but Dave was a rock. Like reporters and CIA operatives, he knew how to protect a source.

I then suggested that a Google search would probably have told him all he needed to know. At which point he produced a series of printouts of various articles I'd written. My bona fides confirmed, I was allowed into the club's main room.

The space was designed for industrial work. Various ducts and pipes crisscrossed the rafters in the forty-foot-high ceiling. The ground was concrete, and one entire wall was a giant garage door.

The four green-felt tables looked a bit odd in a setting where lathes and arc welders would have been more appropriate. But the owners did their best to make the space homey. The walls were painted white and covered with poker-related posters: Stu Ungar, Sam Farha, and other poker greats photographed while playing hands. Sweets and drinks were available for a modest price. A thoroughly palatable pasta dinner was available to all in their full kitchen.

At 7:30 P.M., three of the four tables were busy with $20 "shoot-outs." (Shoot-outs, also known as sit 'n' gos, are single-table tournaments.) The sound of shuffling chips echoed off the walls as the players quietly engaged. It was a young and friendly crowd, college-age mostly, with at least two women at every table. I told Dave that I'd play in the shoot-out that was about to start, gave him $20, and settled into an empty seat. We agreed to speak later, over some $2-$5 pot-limit.

The shoot-out provided lively low-stakes fun. The players pushed their chips in liberally and without much regard to their cards. Each flop brought great excitement and each outcome seemed equally amazing. I managed to finish second. For this honor I was handed an unsealed envelope. Inside was a $20 bill—I got my buy-in back. The letter-sized envelope that accompanied it was clear profit.

These weren't serious gamblers. They were students and working people enjoying a moderate-priced evening of entertainment. With so little at risk, there was no tension in the air, no whining about bad beats, no shouts of triumph. For the first time in weeks, I was feeling expansive. When I moved to the back room to play the $2-$5 game, I sat to the immediate left of Dave and sought to learn more of his background. He owned a couple of businesses before retiring and starting this club.

"I was in insurance," he said. Then he paused for a moment, seeming to communicate that this would be the last we'd talk about his previous careers.

"Insurance," he repeated, "and you can follow that to its logical conclusion."

I then studied the man. In his late fifties, he was still imposingly large, and his deep voice and curt manner led me to wonder what role his intimidating presence played in previous careers. I then thought about potential "logical conclusions" associated with "insurance," and decided just to nod knowingly, as if I had learned all I needed to know.

Dave continued. "Before that, I was in Vietnamese nail salons. . . . And you can follow that to its logical conclusion."

I decided to change the subject. We talked about the poker scene in Virginia and the legal climate that surrounded it. The shoot-outs, he told me, were entirely legal. In Virginia there's no problem in hosting a poker game in a residence as long as no "rake" (house cut) is taken. He then told me about the strange zoning they were able to achieve for the space in which we were playing. The city actually viewed the space as a residence. The owners of the club installed a bedroom, a bathroom, and a kitchen—all municipal requirements for a residence zoning. Dave then pointed to a twentyish dealer across the table and told me that he lived here.

The only revenue-producing game they had was the one in which we were playing. It was raked, and thus fully illegal. I commented that this couldn't be much of a moneymaker. They couldn't clear more than $350-$400 on the table a night. He was taking quite a risk for what must be a modest return. Dave told me with pride that they ran the club for the love of the game.

Dave was full of good information. He warned me to stay clear of mechanics in home games and had one of the dealers—the kid who was living in the space—show me some sleight of hand tricks as a demonstration of what a mechanic could do. In one remarkable exhibition, he placed the red Queens facedown between my tightly squeezed thumb and forefinger. He then made a jabbing motion toward my hand. I felt something, as if he had brushed the cards. He then had me turn over the cards, where I found the black Aces.

Fun. I made a mental note to watch him closely when he returned to dealing.

After seeing the first episode of *Tilt,* the ESPN miniseries written and created by Brian Koppleman and David Levine, the writers of *Rounders,* my mother, deeply concerned, called to ask if the show accurately reflected the poker world. In *Tilt* every character— from top pros to casino management—was cheating. Cards were marked and players were forever passing information by various nefarious means.

I told my mother that despite what she'd seen on TV and in various David Mamet movies, cheating just isn't all that common. The days of mechanics fixing decks have largely passed.

Partly this is because the casinos and underground card rooms I play in supply dealers. None of the players ever touch the cards prior to the deal, and thus never have an opportunity to manipulate the deck. A casino-paid dealer could be working with one of the players around him, but even that would be reasonably difficult to pull off. Dealers must use a very specific shuffle technique: The cards are always visible and never leave the table. A dealer would have to be extremely deft to stack the deck without players' noticing. These days, some casinos use automatic shuffling machines, which make the card order a mystery to everyone, including the dealer.

Other, simpler technologies also help deter cheating. Every club, every casino, and pretty much every serious home game now uses some sort of plastic playing cards, like Kems. They're expensive, about $12 a deck, but they're durable and very difficult to mark. Not impossible, but it takes some work. Most games also use a cut card, a thick opaque plastic sheet the exact size of a playing card that sits beneath the deck. After the shuffle, when the dealer cuts, he places the top half of the deck directly on the cut card. The bottom half is moved to the top, and the dealer picks up the entire stack. With the cut card in place, it's impossible for any of the players or the dealer to know what card is on the bottom of the deck. That makes base dealing—pulling from the bottom of the deck, the most common form of sneaky card manipulation— very difficult. In general, I don't worry about card mechanics. If I've been a dupe for one at some point in the past three years I'd be very surprised.

The greater danger comes from collusion—when two or more players share information and money. Unethical players have devised some sophisticated means for communicating hand strength to their partners—chip placements and hand signals being the most common. A couple of players who are sharing perfect information can manipulate a game. For example, in a fixed-limit hold 'em game, a player could send a specific signal when he has pocket aces. The second player in the team could then put in additional raises with garbage cards, which other people in the hand who weren't part of the team would have to react to. Unsuspecting opponents might end up contributing more bets than they should have.

Collusion happens, and sometimes the perpetrators aren't especially subtle. In the Fourteenth Street club in New York, for example, the most obvious cheaters were a group of players who identified themselves as Gypsies. On any given night early in my poker career, I'd be playing in the $4-$8 game, and the evening would be going in a reasonably typical manner. I'd be winning or losing and chatting with the semifamiliar company. Then, in an avalanche, the Gypsies would descend upon the table. They were friendly—boisterous and chatty. Immediately the size of most pots would balloon, as the Gypsies seemed to be goosing the action by raising one another and dragging along the others who happened to be in the pot. At first I could write off the additional action as a byproduct of the Gypsy equivalent of machismo. These guys seemed to enjoy raising just for the sake of showing up their friends on a big showdown.

After a short while, patterns seemed to develop. In big pots, where one of the Gypsies held a big hand, there always seemed to be another Gypsy in the pot dragging additional bets out of those who were stuck with second-best hands or who were on draws. Eventually, I learned to get up and leave when they came to the table.

A couple of years later, when I was playing as high as $5-$10 no–limit, I spent some time at a midtown club that was owned and frequented by Russians. The club, in a slightly rundown office building, was comfortable but strangely antiseptic. The leather couch, chairs, and felts were all gleaming and new, but on most nights only eight or nine people were playing, and the sounds of clicking chips bounced off the dark, bare walls. One night I found myself in a crazy, action-filled game. There were only nine players, but there was close to $20,000 on the table.

It was a tense night. Pots were big, and at times tempers swelled. The other players, in the heat of the contest, had reverted to Russian, their mother tongue. I didn't mind until I found myself contesting a few large pots. In one hand, I had made a large bluff, and the other player, a short, stocky man whom I knew and liked, was considering a call. Another player, a lanky kid I didn't know, said something in Russian.

"English at the table, please," I said. It's the rule throughout the States, even in a Russian club.

Then he spoke more Russian.

"First of all, one player to a hand. Secondly, English only at the fucking table."

I got the fold I desired, but I was not pleased. I asked the manager if there was an English-only rule, and he agreed and told all assembled to behave.

Less than half an hour later a similar situation developed, but this time I was playing the lanky kid who was talking in Russian earlier, and this time I wanted a call. As soon as he faced my bet, the Russian started. Others responded, clearly offering advice. I was outnumbered, and no one seemed the slightest bit deterred by my earlier show of outrage. I felt I had only one choice: keep my mouth shut and play out the hand. Then leave. I didn't get the call I wanted, and I never went back.


At the Fair Stream Club, while playing $2-$5 pot-limit, I took every possible opportunity to leave the impression in the first hour of play that I was a maniac. In big-bet poker, one ludicrous play is often all a player needs to convince his tablemates he is reckless and a bully. Twice my bluffs were successful and I took down moderate pots without showing my cards. But some at the table were starting to eye me suspiciously.

Then, in late position I was dealt 6♣-8♣ on the button. There were two limpers to me, and I limped along. The big blind raised to twenty, and after two calls, I called as well, as did the small blind. So five players saw the flop. There was a healthy $125 in the pot.

The flop was K♦-J♦-9♥—a total miss for me. It was checked to me on the flop, and I checked along. There was no need to try to bluff into that many players. The turn brought the 4♠. Again, it was checked around. The river was the 8♥, giving me a pair of 8s. The small blind bet out $35. It was folded to me, and I decided to raise to $135.

This was a terrible poker play. I was greedy and careless. If I had a real hand, say Queen-Ten for the straight or King-Jack for two-pair, I surely would have bet the flop or the turn. The possible flush draw (the two diamonds on the flop) made this hand an unlikely candidate for slow-playing. The small blind, to his credit, figured it out and concluded that I was trying to buy the pot. He thought for a while and finally called with nothing more than a nine. I congratulated him on a good read.

I lost $135 on that bet, but that was just fine. I was now seen as a maniac. About a half hour later, I was in the big blind with Queen-2, and flopped bottom two-pair on a board of K-Q-2. I bet $20 on the flop, $60 on the turn, and $100 on the river, and was called on every street by Dave, who was sure his King-9 was the best. On a later hand I flopped a set, and bet out twice and was called.

Later, in a truly remarkable hand, I flopped the nut straight when holding Ten-Jack (a flop of 7♦-8♥-9♦). The first player to act bet out $20, and he was called in two places before it got to me. I raised to $100, not wanting to take any chances with the flush draw. It was folded around to Steve, a delightfully dopey older guy, who fired at pots with the most unlikely hands, like 2-5, then showed the cards just to see the reaction. He called.

The turn was a Ten, and Steve bet $200, leaving only $100 in his stack. I figured that he also had a Jack and we'd be splitting the pot, so I raised him his final $100. He responded "uh-oh," then paused before pushing his final $100 in the pot. He turned over 5-9, and I took down a very nice pot.

I made decent money on the night, about $450, bringing my total poker profit on the trip to just under $2,000. My bankroll stood at just over $17,000. Not horrible, but not where I hoped it to be at this point on the trip. Dave gave me a shirt as a souvenir, and I went on my way.

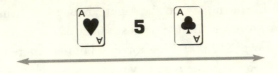

# SOUTH CAROLINA

**T**HERE WERE OTHER GAMES IN THE D.C. AREA, A FRIDAY night $20-$40 limit game at a country club, and a $5-$10 pot-limit game that went off on alternate Sundays. They sounded terrific, loose with a lot of action, and I considered sticking around. But both filled quickly, and getting a seat would be difficult, if not impossible. I also had to consider an ominous weather report. Snow—as much as a half foot of it could fall in northern Virginia. I didn't relish the idea of being snowbound and pokerless in a Hampton Inn a half hour from D.C. It was time to move south.

I phoned my contacts in North Carolina. The Research Triangle area, from all I'd heard, had a lively poker scene. But the same people who a couple of weeks earlier had encouraged me to contact them when in the area were suddenly standoffish. Phone messages went unreturned and e-mails garnered only vague and unhelpful replies. The games, for all I could tell, had suddenly vanished.

I was perplexed until a gregarious fellow in Myrtle Beach called me back and explained the oddities. There'd been a bust in Greensboro. Members of Alcohol Law Enforcement contacted the organizer of a $1,000 buy-in tournament via e-mail. The undercover cops were invited and attended the game. When they confirmed that alcohol was served without a proper license and that people were indeed playing for money—two clear violations of state law—arrests were made and all the money on the premises was seized.

The bust sent a chill through the state's poker world. At the time of my arrival in North Carolina, just two weeks after the arrests, clubs and home games across the state adopted strict rules forbidding new players. If they didn't know you already, there was no way to get in.

A few months after my trip, Greensboro authorities continued their pursuit of poker, this time busting a freeroll—a tournament with no buy-in—at Ham's restaurant. The winners would have received $25 gift certificates and an entry into a later tournament that would award a trip to Vegas. The Ham's arrest spurred an editorial and letters to the editor in the Greensboro *News and Record*. The prevailing opinion seemed to be that law enforcement could find outlets for its energy that better safeguarded the public. There have been no reports of poker-related arrests elsewhere in the state.

With North Carolina essentially dry, I drove on to South Carolina, where I had a game lined up outside of Greenville, a small city in the western portion of the state. My familiarity with one Greenville institution, Bob Jones University, made me wary of the place. In 2000, then–Texas governor George W. Bush stopped at the fundamentalist Christian school for a campaign speech. He didn't seem to mind that school rules banned interracial dating. The appearance drew national media attention, with many questioning why a presidential candidate would implicitly endorse such values. In attempts to quell the outrage that accompanied the publicity, the school claimed that their ban wasn't racist at all but promoted a larger principle. Genetic blending, it argued, leads to a "one worldism," the consequences of which are truly horrible. As Bob Jones III stated on *Larry King Live,* "We stand against the one-world government, against the coming world of the Antichrist, which is a one-world system of blending, of all differences, of blending of national differences, economic differences, church differences, into one big ecumenical world." If I followed the logic correctly, then Bob Jones III believes segregation keeps the Antichrist at bay.

The ban was lifted the day of the Larry King interview, but it lived in my memory as I drove into town.

At first glimpse, Greenville seemed a simple, compact city in the midst of a well-planned downtown renewal project. Eight blocks of Main Street were lined with recently built stores and restaurants; the wide, attractive sidewalks accommodated ample outdoor seating. A couple of condo complexes were in the late stages of construction, and fliers in retailers' windows advertised cultural events around the city: plays, museum exhibitions, music performances. The city was creating a charming, walkable alternative to suburbia. When I saw that the sidewalks were not inscribed with verses from Revelations, the remnants of my dread dissipated.

I'd split the drive from Virginia into two days and had spent the previous night in a highway-side hotel. The game I'd set up in Greenville wasn't for another day, but I was restive and wanted some action. So I found a coffee shop with a decent dark roast and free Internet access. I fired up my Web browser and quickly found a relatively small pot-limit game and e-mailed the organizer. He called me within an hour and seemed enthusiastic to have me come. I had a game for the night.

I imagine that when viewed from my parents' vantage, my life has appeared to be a series of abrupt stops and starts. My first destination after college was Los Angeles, where I was determined to make it as a comedy writer. Looking back, it was a silly goal, as I despised situation comedies. But I was convinced my talents were so overwhelming that they would transcend my hatred of the form. Three years of mediocre scripts and near-pointless meetings was all I could endure, and I headed to the Sangre de Cristo Mountains of New Mexico, Taos, for a year of outdoor adventure—hiking, rafting, skiing.

My college girlfriend and I rekindled our relationship then, and she moved out to New Mexico. A few months later we called family to say we had eloped. We moved to San Francisco a year later and my career changed to technology. After five years there, we moved to New York and divorced. Concurrent with these shifts was a multitude of projects, some successful, most aborted. I started one business, abandoned others, wrote several scripts, and cowrote-produced-directed a short film.

I can only imagine the breathlessness and worry my family suffered as I elucidated my ever-changing focus. There was no grad school, no coherent path. Plus a quick marriage after a difficult courtship. I'd guess the phrase "bad choices" was used in family circles more than once.

During one low period when I seemed especially rudderless, my father, a proven entrepreneur, made efforts to ease my entry into a franchise business. I wanted nothing to do with it. My refusal was regretfully bitter and vehement. I was determined to continue on my path—whatever the hell that was.

Then there was poker, which must have provoked a variety of fears. My folks would naturally worry for my physical and financial safety and my ability to maintain a relationship while living as a gambler. The specter of addiction must also have caused concern. One side of my family has a history of alcoholism, and for much of my adult life, I watched as the sober, responsible relatives struggled to contain the swath of damage the addictive behaviors wrought.

I could tell my mother and father that I was fine, a poker enthusiast who could and would walk away from the game if it ever became an undue burden. To prove my lack of propensity for addiction I could tell them that I spent a good deal of my college days drunk and high and that during those years nearly every drug that crossed my path found its way into my bloodstream. But as I transitioned to a more adult existence, I gave it all up. Years could go by between tokes on a joint, and the absence didn't bother me in the least. I might drink a couple of beers on a Friday, but that's about all I ever want.

Somehow I didn't think I'd be comforting my mother by saying, "You know, I used to get up and do bong hits. Now I don't." I'd have to let my actions speak for themselves. I hoped that in time, as I succeeded in this endeavor, my parents would come to think of my choice as odd and risky, but reasonable for someone with a history of wanderlust and a need for experimentation.

But my parents probably wouldn't have given much thought to another wearing aspect of poker: loneliness. In the course of the trip, I was surrounded by people who were alien to me and to each other. The halting small talk that repeated itself at tables— the recitations of towns of origins and lines of work—was tiresome. I often craved more meaningful interactions, and I was hopeful that the game I was headed to in Greenville would offer some relief. I expected deeper discussions and familiar laughs. I'd be a spectator to the true warmth, but at least the milieu would be comforting.

With a six-pack of Heineken in hand, I knocked on the door of a modest ranch house just outside of downtown Greenville. The street was crowded; similar houses lined both sides of the street, and massive pickup trucks occupied almost every driveway. Secondary cars, with two wheels on grass and two on pavement, sat along the street. The door swung open and I was greeted by chaos. A sheltie ran toward me while barking his most menacing bark. The sounds of a shoot-'em-up video game blared on an unseen television. The floor was littered with toys. A young weary-looking

woman with an unkempt head of wiry hair stood silently
before me.

"I'm sorry. I think I'm at the wrong house. I was here for a
poker game."

"No, this is it," she said, her look of exhaustion unwavering.

I entered and was led to the dining room, where seven people
were spread around a poker table. I was introduced to the group
and sat. I asked about the buy-in and was told that $40 was the av-
erage stack. The game was smaller than I thought, but it didn't
matter much. I peeled off two twenties and sat down.

After a few hands of play a man across the table made the common inquiries—where I was from, what I did. I told him, and
then the table slipped into silence. I asked similar questions of the
others and they answered and then quiet once again overtook the
table. I offered beer to those assembled, but no one was interested.

I saw that Pete, the twenty-something with black hair in a long
ponytail, was dealing every hand, and I offered to share those du-
ties with him. He was fine, he said. It was then that I noticed that
Pete was dealing but not playing. It took me another ten minutes
to realize that Pete was raking pots, taking a dollar or two from
each hand dealt. This wasn't a friendly home game at all, I realized. It was Pete's business, and the other players were as unfamiliar to each other as they were to me.

Pete's wife, the woman who had answered the door, sat in for
some hands, but she had little energy for the game or the people at
the table. Her son, an adorable but wan child, came to the table in
need of his mother's attention. He didn't feel well, he said. She
kissed him and stroked his head and took him on frequent trips
to the bathroom. During one bathroom run, Pete told me that
it was the chemotherapy that bothered his stomach so much.
Leukemia.

I nodded and cashed out early. The game offered nothing I
wanted.

---

I managed to get a cheap room at the Greenville Hyatt Regency, which was at one end of Main Street. When I returned to the hotel, the lobby was filled with spectacularly outfitted teens. I entered a glass elevator with young women in gorgeous evening gowns. Pimply young men in tails followed.

I turned to the nearest young woman, whose gown was made of broad bands of black and gold, and asked, "Why is everyone so dressed up?"

"A deb ball," she replied, smiling.

"Deb ball?"

"Debutante's ball," she replied patiently.

I nodded. I'd never been to a deb ball and was unsure what one asks at the conclusion of such an affair. "How did it go?" I managed.

"Fun."

I smiled. I'm sure it was.

Once in my hotel room, I did what over a hundred thousand poker players do every night: got on the Internet and logged on to my favorite cyber poker room. Within a minute I had $1,000 in front of me as I played a $5–$10 no-limit game. The money was real—my checking account was linked to Neteller, an online money-transfer agent. From Neteller I could move money in and out of various poker sites or back to my checking account.

The virtual table was viewed from above, as if a camera hovering ten feet over the action was transmitting the image to my computer. At the table, crudely animated characters occupied crudely drawn chairs, and below each character a player's name—his "handle"—was printed in large block letters. At the start of a deal, the button was moved, blinds were posted, and hole cards were dealt. The game proceeded like every game of hold 'em does. The only difference is that instead of speaking my action or moving chips, I'd press a button that said "raise," "fold," or "call."

Most online players won't play a no-limit game with a $1,000 buy-in—it's too big a game. But with dozens of poker sites and hundreds of thousands of players worldwide contributing to their accounts, game selection on the Internet is terrific. That night there were probably twenty or thirty $5-$10 no-limit games I was aware of. If I played smaller—say $2-$4 limit hold 'em—there would be hundreds of tables to chose from.

I'd opted for a shorthanded game, a table where only five players were involved. I love shorthanded play. With fewer players holding cards, one can be less wary of monster starting hands— pocket Aces or Kings—and thus raise preflop with a wider selection of hole cards. And with blinds coming around so frequently, simply surrendering the big blind every time there's a raise can get costly. If a particular player is continually raising my blind, I may have to pop him back with nothing at all, just to let him know that my blinds are not there to be stolen. Generally, aggression plays a bigger role in shorthanded games, and that makes it a lot of fun. Sadly, there are very few short-handed games in casinos and card rooms as it's a poor use of manpower to have one dealer servicing four or five players.

At many online poker sites the same people come to the same tables continually, and over time I can learn their styles of play. I don't have to commit everyone's every move to memory, though. All sites include a *notes* feature, which allows me to type in and store any observations I've made. Each time a player with notes appears at my table, the jottings I previously typed accompany him.

There were a couple of players at my table that night with notes I'd previously made, plus a couple I'd never seen before. New players—whether live or online—require a fair amount of study. You never know when you're going to end up playing a big pot against a player you know little about. If you're to have any idea of how best to proceed, you must be paying attention to the minutiae of less-eventful hands. Hopefully, you'll quickly draw some broad conclusions about a new opponent's abilities and tendencies.

I was looking very closely at the guy on my left. This guy had a big stack—over $1,800—and from the way he played, I guessed he'd gotten very lucky before my arrival. He was committing a lot of money at times when it was clearly inappropriate. After about five minutes I decided he was a "calling station"—a player who doesn't raise and doesn't fold, just calls street after street after street. There's no player type that's easier to beat. Just wait for a solid hand and bet—and bet and bet. Sure enough, a few minutes later, the calling station gave away about $900 after calling an opponent down with pocket 6s. My mouth was watering.

Shortly after this giveaway, I was dealt 2♥-5♥ in the big blind. If there had been any raise at all, I would have folded. But with two limpers to me, I was able to see the flop without committing another dollar. And it was stunning: 4♦-3♥-6♦. I'd flopped a straight—2-3-4-5-6. With two diamonds on board, though, I needed to be cautious, but I also wanted to get some value. I checked, and the calling station bet the minimum: $10. The other player in the hand called, and I raised to $80. Both players, to my surprise, called the $80. Now I had to assume that at least one of them was on the diamond draw. The turn was the T♥—about as good a card as I could see. I bet $280, the exact size of the pot. The calling station did what calling stations always do, and the third player, to my utter amazement, moved in—he raised me almost $600. I called instantly and the calling station did as well. The river was the 8♥, giving me a low flush.

The fish showed 6♣-4♠, for two-pair. The third player, A♦-9♦. He'd pushed all his money in on a diamond flush draw and missed.

Over $2,000 that these guys had labored for, banked, and then moved to their online accounts was now mine. In the comfort of a pillowtop bed in a room at the Hyatt Regency, I'd taken my biggest pot of the trip.

The next day I met with Jack, who was taking me to a no-limit game that night that he said was very juicy. I'd met Jack through an Internet discussion forum, and prior to lunch that day at a chain restaurant in Anderson, we'd never spoken. All contact was through e-mail.

Jack had a cared-for exterior. His hair was short and neatly cropped, and he wore a nifty leather jacket that hung comfortably on his slight frame. His eyes were a piercing hazel. When the waitress delivered the check, she included her name and phone number, either ignoring or failing to notice Jack's wedding band.

"Looks like you made a friend," I said, pointing to the jotting.

"Oh, yeah," he said, and laughed, leaving the check on the table as we left.

We chatted about the poker scene in Greenville and South Carolina as a whole. I told him of the game I had played the previous night. He agreed it was both weird and creepy. He was familiar with one of the players, Tim. Word around town was that Tim had fled from a pool hall after compiling a sizable debt. Tim was no longer welcome around area gamblers.

The conversation naturally shifted to gamblers' ethics. We both commented on how unusual Tim was, how rare it is to find a serious gambler who won't honor his debts. It is remarkable, we agreed, how amazingly trustworthy poker players are. We recounted tales of opponents who'd let us know we were exposing our hole cards or insisted on a proper count of pot, even when the mistake was in their favor.

I inquired how gambling was thought of here at the buckle of the Bible Belt, the home of Bob Jones University. Predictably, gamblers are not highly regarded by fundamentalist Christians.

But Jack had little patience for the "Holy Rollers" he met at work and in other parts of his life. "Those people talk about being moral, but you can't trust them for a second," he said.

The game that night was deep within a suburban subdivision outside of Greenville. I followed Jack's taillights through a series of turns until we arrived at a driveway and parked. I wondered how long it would take me to get out of this landmarkless maze. The interior of the house was spartan: a leather couch, chair, and television wasn't nearly enough furniture for the large living room, and the walls were mostly bare. The residents either hadn't been there long or were leaving soon, I guessed.

We gathered around the poker table. The group was young, with all but one of the players in their midtwenties. We were playing $1-$2 no-limit, a game where there can be some decent money on the table, so it could be worth my while. But I nearly sighed aloud when a couple of the players bought in for less than $100. With stacks in place, three players, including Jack, put on mirrored sunglasses.

As play got under way, two players discussed the previous evening's activities.

"I went to a party at the Hyatt," said the host, a car salesman still wearing his dress shirt and tie. "When I got there, there was only"—he halted briefly, as if measuring the advisability of uttering the next words—"fucking niggers."

He paused, his eyes darting from one acquaintance to another. He received only blank expressions in reply. No one, including myself, conveyed disgust. But there was no sign of approval in the faces around him either. The words floated in the air for a moment, no one wishing to be associated with them. The host went on with his story.

An hour into the game, I was having a hard time maintaining interest. At one point I raised with 7♠-8♠ suited, only to see Jack reraise big from the blinds. Looking for a reason to emerge from my stupor, I called. I flopped the flush draw, called off the rest of my money on the flop, then hit a spade, cracking Jack's Aces.

One of the sunglass-wearing players chewed tobacco at the table and deposited the brown refuse into a clear water bottle, which he held before him. When we exchanged some small talk and I mentioned my hometown, he called me a "fucking Yankee," in a tone that was at most half-joking.

I half-smiled and turned away. I was unsettled and played a few orbits after that, then left with a $100 profit.

The fish in this town were either too small or too hard to find for me to bother wasting any more time here.

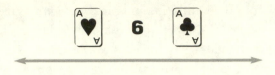

# 6

# GEORGIA

WHEN MARISA AND I MET, I COULD MOST ACCURATELY DE-scribe my profession as technology writer. I was independent, a consultant to high-tech companies and the author of a couple of books on moderately arcane topics. (*MySQL/PHP Database Applications* is a rollicking read!) She taught third grade in the South Bronx. By the time she moved in with me two years later, I'd given up on technology completely; poker and poker writing were my sole sources of income. During the transition, she voiced no qualms about my developing line of work, offered no reproofs. Over time, she seemed to view the ever-growing magnitude of my wins and loses with wonderment, but never concern.

It was easy for her, in part, I think, because her large, Italian family had a history with cards—nickel-dime games during summer retreats at Cape Cod, occasional gin rummy matches between aunts. And some in her family simply liked to gamble. Uncle Bobby, a lovely and gregarious man, gleefully recounted stories of his high-rolling trips to Atlantic City at parties. Grandma loved the slots and with little provocation would pull out her Foxwoods Wampum Card as proof. During my first Christmas with the family, she grabbed the card from her purse to show me. In reply, I pulled my own Wampum Card from my wallet. We then passed a pleasant quarter hour dealing out five-card draw hands.

Even absent that history, I think Marisa would have been OK with my new career. She's a true optimist, and she trusts me. I imagine she'd be pleased with any path I chose that showed the slightest hint of success. She encouraged my trips to World Poker Tour events. When our nightly activities—hers spent at writing classes and playing violin in a community orchestra, mine at poker clubs—kept us from seeing one another days in a row, she'd often fall asleep on the couch so that I was sure to wake her when I returned from a session of cards. When I conceived of and planned the three-month cross-country trip, she was nothing but supportive.

Not every would-be pro has a companion like Marisa. A skeptical mate, one incapable of viewing the daily swings with the necessary detachment can—and probably should—halt an aspiring professional before he's aware of his true abilities. The stress is simply too much for most to bear.

I talked with a top pro—one of the most consistent winners among high-stakes players and a father to three children—about the difficulty he had with his spouse. He said that it took him a while to understand how tough it was on her, but after a couple of years he learned that the best thing he could do was isolate her from the short-term stresses of the game. He wouldn't even tell her about the wins, because, he pointed out, those are stressful in their own way. He went to work, and when he returned, he kept the difficulties of his workday to himself, like any good professional family man. It didn't help especially; he divorced and thinks that the poker life had a lot to do with it. But he still thought this was the right way to go.

When I phoned Marisa after arriving in Atlanta, I saw how badly I was managing this part of my life. In the course of the trip, she'd already talked me off tilt once and endured a couple of bad-beat stories. Sometime after the trip, she said to me, "On the phone, I could tell by the way you said hello how you were doing."

That was simply unfair to her. Though she seemed to have a bottomless reserve of patience for my frailties, this couldn't continue. I could not let this profession become a burden to her.

Anchors on the Weather Channel spoke in solemn, urgent tones as they probed their regional correspondents about the seriousness of the situation. The correspondents replied with furrowed brows and narrated taped segments that showed hooded and parka-clad pedestrians hurriedly moving through the streets. The anchors then introduced a series of maps—satellite images, sketches of the country covered with multicolored bands. Each reinforced one inescapable conclusion: It was cold.

A series of low-pressure systems loaded with bitter arctic air swept from Canada, through the Midwest, and continued unabated to the South. Memphis had been enveloped, South Carolina had seen one of the worst stretches in its history, and when I arrived in Atlanta, I saw that I would not be escaping frosty days there. I shivered through Atlanta Underground, a horribly insulated, second-rate mall, in a failed attempt to kill a few hours before checking in to my hotel. Once in my room, I kept my coat and scarf around me as the long-dormant heater battled the deep chill that permeated the space. Atlanta, I concluded, doesn't do cold especially well.

But it had an active poker scene, from what I'd heard, and I had a game lined up in the northern part of the city. The directions to the club led me through downtown and into suburbia, about twenty minutes north of the city. After a few turns I found myself in a garden-apartment complex of about fifteen modest two-story buildings. I parked by the pool, in one of the many spots marked "Guest," and made my way to building D. I entered into a hallway where I could see doorways for two apartments. Above the door on my right, a security camera was perched on the frame. I buzzed the door below the camera, announced my name, and was allowed to enter.

A young man talking on a cell phone opened the door and waved me in. The unit was like dozens of others I'd seen in large, cheap suburban apartment complexes across the country. The moderately sized rooms, durable brown carpet, and small patio with a sliding glass door offered meager luxuries. It was the kind of place you move into and initially feel it's nice enough—clean and reasonably comfortable. In four months the charmlessness wears on you and you're looking to get the hell out.

But there were no residents in this apartment; this space was meant for business. The living room held two sleek poker tables, the dining room another two. The tables were casino quality, with a cutout for a dealer's rack and a drop box where the rake would be deposited. On a wall, a dry-erase board listed high-hand jackpots and a small LED message board flashed the current bad-beat jackpot: $9,000.* One bedroom served as an office, and the other as a lounge of sorts, with a couch and a TV.

I was early, the first player for the night, and had little choice but to sit quietly at one of the poker tables until some other players arrived. I saw that three young men, all college age and dressed in business-casual clothes, ran the place. They moved about the space with an efficiency that showed the seriousness with which they approached this venture. They brushed the felts, talked with each other about small problems they'd encountered in previous days, and reminded each other of coming obligations. They were proud first-time entrepreneurs.

I called to one of the young men, who wore a crisp dress shirt and jeans. Like any good business owner, he had time for a new client, and he immediately sat across the table from me. I asked

---

* A bad-beat jackpot is awarded when a particularly big hand loses a pot. Normally, the losing hand must be Aces full of Jacks or better. The jackpot is usually split among the players at the table, with the loser of the hand receiving the largest percentage. To feed the jackpot, card rooms pull a dollar from every hand played.

about the club's history. It had to be relatively new. With only this provocation he launched into a recitation of the club's competitive advantages.

"We have the biggest bad-beat jackpot in the Atlanta area," he told me. "Over $9,000. And we now have tournaments going every weekend and three days during the week. This is quickly becoming the best club in Atlanta," he finished, his eye contact lingering.

"Great."

"We're also very security conscious," he offered.

"Yeah, I noticed the camera in the hallway. Did the neighbors say anything when that went in?"

"No, not at all."

"That doesn't seem possible. How about the management? They must have noticed."

"Haven't heard a thing," he said with a smile. "And there are other security features in place."

"Like what?"

He didn't answer.

"You got guns?"

"Just know that you're safe. Excuse me," he said and walked away. If he had stuck around for another minute I might have told him that, contrary to his intent, our discussion had left me quite fearful.


For years, Doyle Brunson, Brian "Sailor" Roberts, and "Amarillo Slim" Preston made their living traveling the roads of Texas, moving from game to game. Along the way they were held up— hijacked, they called it—dozens of times. They had shotguns pointed at their heads and were left tied up on the sides of rural roads while thieves sped away with their money. In *Poker Wisdom of a Champion,* a collection of essays where Brunson uses anecdotes from his life to illustrate vital poker concepts, he tells of a Texas robbery that occurred after an ostentatious companion flashed a thick wad of hundreds at a lunch stop. The lesson: Don't flash thick wads at lunch stops and stay the hell away from people who do.

Players in places like West Texas or Atlanta or New York know that they're operating underground. The clubs are mostly clean and professionally managed, but players know that no matter what happens within the club's confines, the cops will not be called. Does this add a little risk to a player's night? Sure. But when I head out to a $2-$5 no-limit game with $1,500 in my pocket, I know that bad beats or my own reckless play are far more likely to wipe me out than a group of gunmen.

Still, in these days when ubiquitous ATMs dole out cash $60 at a time and 7-Elevens take credit cards, poker players are among the last great stickup prospects for ambitious thieves. Even in places where poker is entirely legal and aboveground, players have endured harrowing experiences. In *Super System 2,* Brunson tells of a home-invasion robbery that occurred at his Las Vegas house during the World Series of Poker. Normally, Brunson said, he doesn't carry cash, but that night he had "big chips. Lots of them."

When confronted with a gun, Brunson feigned a heart attack. But this didn't slow his attackers down. When his alarm system sounded, he was pistol-whipped and his nose was broken. At that point, as Brunson tells it:

> *The phone rang.*
>
> *"That's the alarm company," one of the men growled. "Tell them everything's all right or we'll kill you right now!"*
>
> *It was, indeed, the security company, responding to a standard alert. In order to determine whether this was a false alarm, they asked for a password that would let then know everything was okay.*

*Louise [Doyle's wife] took the call and had the presence of mind to give the wrong password, just as I had given the wrong codes. But instead of picking up on the clue that something was terribly amiss at the Brunson residence, the woman on the other end admonished Louise, saying she had been given the wrong password.*

*"Yes, I know," Louise confirmed politely, hoping the intruders wouldn't divine the direction of the phone conversation. She again repeated the invalid code and hung up. Now, you'd think that was enough to send help on its way. But no. The phone rang again. And again it was the security company. This time one of the robbers answered and tried, pathetically, to sound like a woman. He was told that the code previously given is invalid. Belatedly, the agent got suspicious and figured it out. Finally, she hung up and called the police.*

*Slamming the phone down, the robber lost his cool, charged back into the room where the other bandit had a gun to my head. "Don't kill him, kill me!" It was my dear Louise's voice. When the man had stepped back from me, she had jumped between me and the gun.*

The gunmen fled shortly after with some of Doyle's chips.

In early 2005, Greg Raymer was accosted in what most would assume was among the safest places in the poker world: in the hallway outside his room at the Bellagio Hotel on the Las Vegas Strip. Raymer was in town for a tournament, but that night he had been playing in a big cash game. After the session, he put his money in his safe-deposit box and took the elevator to his room. Another man was in the elevator, and they exited on the same floor. Raymer went one way, the man the other. At the entrance to his room, Raymer saw another man struggling with his card key. He thought nothing of it, until the man in the elevator suddenly appeared. At once the two were upon him, demanding that he go into the room.

But Raymer knew that his room was outside the view of security cameras, and refused. In there, he thought, he could be killed. He fought, knocking one of the men down. A gun appeared, but Raymer didn't stop struggling. He yelled for security and used his heavy frame to batter the men. Finally, they fled. When discussing the incident on a popular message board, Raymer wrote: "If it weren't for the gun, I would've chased them down the hallway, and smashed their faces in as they waited for the elevator.

"These guys were five nine and six three, and combined out-weighed me by a lot (the tall guy was a lot bigger than me). Yet I still beat them off, and came out of this with no injuries other than a slight abrasion on one shoulder.

"I don't write this to brag, I just want any robbery-minded people out there who hear about this to know that I'm a tough mark, and they won't get that much off me even if they succeed. And if they do succeed, they'll either go to jail, or I'll find them myself and make them wish they'd gone to jail. I'm a very nice guy, super-easygoing, and am friends with pretty much everybody I meet, but if you f*ck with my life or my family, I'm going to f*ck you back and then some."

One of the men who held up Raymer was a poker player, and was quickly recognized by Bellagio security. The assailants were found and arrested.

Both Brunson and Raymer have made one point absolutely clear: They don't carry cash and you won't find any in their houses. It's obviously a wise strategy, but one I couldn't employ on the trip. I needed to keep a fair amount of cash on hand, just to make sure I could get through a few losing nights, and I didn't want the hassle of pulling money in and out of the bank every time I arrived and left a new location. Generally, the first thing I'd do when I got to a town was check into a hotel and get a safe-deposit box. I'd only keep on me what I'd need for a night's play.

But there were still nervous moments. I never knew quite what to do with my thick wad of $100s at those times when I stopped for lunch or arrived in a town before check-in. Leave it in the car? Cars are stolen all the time. Keep it in my front pocket? I'd been held up before, and it could happen again.

Just after arriving in Atlanta, I decided to do some sightseeing, and at that time I was working under the philosophy that I was best off with the money on me. So I headed out into the Atlanta streets with $6,300 in my front left pocket. When I found myself lost in a desolate alley, I felt far more panicky than a New Yorker ought to in such situations. Shortly after that, I divided the bills into three smaller bundles. One I kept under the front seat, one in the trunk, and one in my pocket. It wasn't a great plan, but it was the best I could think to devise.

If I ever started to book significant wins on the trip, the bulk of bills could be a real problem, but at this point I was safe from that inconvenience.

Once the game in the Atlanta club got started, I understood why security was on the club owner's mind. There had been a spate of armed robberies in the weeks before I arrived, and it was all the assembled players could talk about. The most recent robbery had occurred just a few days before, when masked gunmen stormed a house that was hosting a tournament. All the players were relieved of their cash and jewelry. Best guess was that the robbers got away with more than $10,000. But the police were never called, as the men who ran the tournament were not interested in getting arrested so soon after getting robbed.

I played two nights at the apartment club. The players were clean-cut professionals—a couple of engineers, a banker, a restaurateur—who were uniformly friendly. The first night I applied the same techniques that worked so well for me in Philadelphia and Virginia. I bullied the table and was caught on a bluff early. I then hit a couple of hands and got paid nicely. The second night, however, went badly. And it was the first time on the trip when I was unable to assess the quality of my own play. Looking at my notes describing a few of the hands a couple of months later, I didn't know what lessons I could learn.

On one hand halfway through the evening, I raised to $25 in late position with 6♦-7♦. The player to my left and a blind both called. The flop—5♣-8♦-K♥—gave me the straight draw (any 9 or 4 would give me the nut straight). I led at the pot, betting $60. I would have been perfectly happy if my opponents thought I had Ace-King and folded. The player to my left squirmed a bit and after a moment of thought made what I determined to be a very reluctant call. He seemed worried that the cards he held were going to get him in a lot of trouble. The blind folded. I figured that the caller had a King with a mediocre kicker, maybe King-Ten. The turn was the 2♦, leaving the board 5♣-8♦-K♥-2♦. I now had a diamond flush draw to go along with my straight draw.

My stack was fairly short at that time so I went all-in for a slight overbet of the pot: $210. It seemed like a good move. I could win, I thought, if any 4, 9, or diamond hit on the river; any one of fifteen cards would make me a stellar hand. Or I could take it down if my opponent decided that I, indeed, had Ace-King and folded. This sort of move—betting with a hand that is not best but can easily improve is known as a "semi-bluff." My opponent thought and thought and thought, and finally called. He then flipped over K♦-4♦. Not only did he have the best hand, he killed my diamond draw. The J♥ on the river gave my opponent the pot.

This is a hand where I clearly didn't need to go to battle. I didn't need to raise preflop, I didn't need to bet on the flop, or move in on the turn. Many competent players might look at this description and say, "You lost $300 on a garbage hand that was in serious trouble on every street. Why get yourself in that situation?"

But there's another way to look at this: If my opponent didn't have a King, he would have folded on the flop. And if the turn wasn't a diamond, I probably would have cut my losses, checked, and folded to a decent bet. Finally, if my opponent hadn't picked up a diamond draw of his own on the turn, he might have folded to my all-in bet had I decided to go that route. In short, an unlikely distribution of cards both kept me in the hand and saw that I'd lose. To me that sounds like bad luck. On the other hand, it's hard to claim bad luck when you lose with a hand like 6-7. Maybe I did a poor job of evaluating the risk. I really don't know which it was.

Several hands went badly that night and I lost $900, which put me $200 in the red for my time in the Peach State. My profit on the trip at this point was just over $3,400. My bankroll was at $18,200. I wasn't making the sort of progress that would allow me to play the $10-$20 when I got to Commerce. I was starting to wonder if my plans were too ambitious, if the trip would culminate with a game that was no higher than the ones I started with. But there was time. If I tightened up my game and saw some better cards, I could make the $20,000. I knew it was possible.

The Atlanta poker landscape changed radically a few months after my visit. In February 2005, the Gwinnett County Multi-Agency Drug Task Force raided a poker game held at a house outside Atlanta. Everyone—the players and the managers—were forced facedown on the floor as the cops swept through with their automatic weapons and SWAT gear. Everyone was arrested. The players were charged with misdemeanors, the organizers with felonies. A deputy from a neighboring county who was supplying armed security was also arrested on felony counts. According to some accounts, the players were held in jail for over twenty hours without access to phones.

Soon after the arrest, I got the following e-mail from the Atlanta club I attended.

*Our apologies,*

*Due to recent events, the club will be closed indefinitely.*

*We hope to return in a better, safer, and favorable form. All of us appreciate your friendship, loyalty, and support over the past year. As always, your questions and input are welcome.*

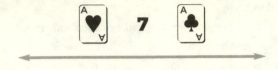

# 7

# BILOXI

CHRISTMAS WAS FAST APPROACHING AND I HAD TO FIGURE out where I'd spend the holiday. As an atheist of Jewish heritage, Christmas presented no religious obligations. I just wanted to make sure I could find a game, and Atlanta wasn't looking too promising. I called a couple of people I'd met in the area, but when I told them of my quest for Noël gambling, they were no help. One guy I'd met in the Atlanta club commented that poker sounded like a nice reprieve from his wife's family and I got to telling him nostalgically about New York, where many of the clubs are up and running on Christmas Day. Jews—and there are a few of them in the metropolitan area—are notoriously bored and in need of diversion on Christmas. Poker offers one of the few alternatives to movies and Chinese food.

"Jews eat Chinese food on Christmas?" he asked.

"Yeah," I replied. "Those are the only restaurants open."

"Huh," he said, clearly finding this a notable piece of cultural trivia. "I think I'd like being a Jew."

I laughed and suggested he conceal the motives for his conversion from his rabbi.

It looked as though I'd need to travel to one of the places within driving distance that had legal casino gambling. There were some dog tracks in Florida that had Texas hold 'em, but Florida law limited bets on all rounds to $2. I imagined that a $2 max Christmas Day game at a dog track would be unbearably depressing. My other options were in Mississippi, which had two casino towns. In the northern part of the state, just outside of Memphis, was Tunica, which is known to have a great poker scene. But from what I'd heard, Tunica was at its best when the World Poker Tour was in town, and that was in January. My plan was to head there shortly after the New Year for a lengthy stay. The only other option was Biloxi, which sat on Mississippi's Gulf Coast. I didn't know much about the town, but some Internet research showed that there were at least a couple of casinos with poker rooms. So Biloxi it was.

The seven-hour drive through most of Alabama brought no relief from the frigid weather. When I caught sight of the Gulf of Mexico, the temperature, a radio voice told me, was thirty-four degrees. The voice also noted that the entire Gulf Coast, from Houston to Tallahassee, was suffering historically bad winter weather. A white Christmas in New Orleans was a distinct possibility.

I was worn out from the drive and decided to settle into the first casino I encountered, which happened to be the Imperial Palace. The IP employed a vague Polynesian-tropical theme. There were palm trees outside the front entrance and the dealers wore Hawaiian shirts. On this day the hotel lobby was roughly forty-five degrees; septuagenarians at the nickel slots wore parkas, and the table-games dealers looked miserable in their short sleeves. Tahiti this was not.


Gambling came to Biloxi and neighboring Gulfport when, in 1990, the Mississippi legislature passed a bill allowing "dockside" gaming. This gave counties along the Mississippi River and Gulf Coast the right to legalize gambling within their jurisdictions as long as the casinos were located over water. This odd restriction was a concession to antigambling legislators who wanted to ensure that legalized gambling could not spread throughout the state. By the end of 1992 four casinos had dropped moorings into Gulf waters and hoisted full-service casinos atop them. The attached hotels were built on dry ground. By the end of 1995, the area had more square feet of casino space than any place in the country outside of Las Vegas.

But casino operators in the area never expected to compete directly with Vegas. Travelers from Chicago or Seattle or Fargo who sought the luxuries of the Venetian or the spectacle of the Luxor wouldn't consider southern Mississippi a viable vacation spot. But gamblers from surrounding cities like Mobile, Tallahassee, and New Orleans needed a nearby, modestly priced spot to blow a few discretionary dollars.

The casinos ably catered to the market's needs, offering the low-stakes gambling and cheap food that locals craved. According to the Harrison County Development Commission, the average casino visitor lived a short drive away and found his way to Biloxi-Gulfport 13.4 times per year. Overall, gambling added over $3 billion annually to the local economy, helping drive up desperately low incomes and housing prices. In 2002, median house prices in Harrison County reached $115,000, doubling where it was ten years earlier.

Not all the casinos thrived. In 1999, Steve Wynn, the hotel and resort visionary behind the Mirage, Bellagio, and, most recently, Las Vegas's opulent Wynn, opened the Beau Rivage in Biloxi. The resort was unmistakably upscale, with a refined interior design and high-end restaurants. An early ad campaign featured a voice-over by Elizabeth Taylor and said that the Beau Rivage would bring "class" to the area. But the hotel floundered. Locals weren't interested in the relatively expensive rooms and tight slots that accompany such class. Beau Rivage was a drag on MGM Mirage's corporate profits until strategies were rethought. When I drove the roads around Biloxi, billboards advertised the Beau Rivage's penny slots and the expanded buffet.

Those advertisements, the casinos, and just about everything else in the area were devastated by Hurricane Katrina in September 2005, ten months after my visit. Whole neighborhoods were leveled, and in one of the most remarkable images following the disaster, the Gulfport Grand Casino was lifted by the storm surge into the middle of a nearby street. The casinos pledged to rebuild, this time aided by amended state laws that allowed them to construct their gambling halls on solid ground. But it will likely be years before the reconstruction is complete enough for the area to again become a regional draw. Only then will the gaming industry provide the jobs and tax revenue that lifted the area out of some of the country's most intense poverty.

That Christmas Eve, I went to the Biloxi Grand, which I was told had the largest poker room in the South, with about fifteen tables. The games were tiny; $1-$4-$8-$8 limit hold 'em, a version of the game I'd never before seen or heard of, was the most popular choice. That night, the biggest game was $15-$30 limit. I asked about no-limit or pot-limit games and was told that I might catch one on Christmas. But even that was unlikely, and for now limit hold 'em was my only choice.

Limit poker is essentially a game of math in which the best players are forever analyzing statistics and making decisions accordingly. To an extent this is true of all poker, but in most low- or medium-stakes limit games the other factors associated with quality play—psychological manipulation, hand reading, fearlessness—are subordinate to mathematics. There's one very simple reason for this: In limit hold 'em, bluffing almost never works.

A quick example shows why this is the case. Say that you're playing a $5-$10 limit hold 'em game, where the bets and raises preflop and on the flop are $5, and the bets and raises on the turn and river are $10. If you were to raise preflop with Ace-King, you'd likely be called by a player who held pocket 10s. On a flop of something like 2♦-7♣-4♠, you might bet and hope to take down the small pot. But it's hard to imagine that anyone would fold for a $5 bet while holding an overpair to the board. Now, imagine the turn is the 8♠, and you make the $10 turn bet. At this point, with the blinds and previous action, your opponent would be looking at a pot of $47, and it would cost only $10 to call. Getting almost 5 to 1 on his money, this guy *should* call, even if he thinks there's a reasonable chance you have pocket Kings. The potential reward easily justifies the risk. If the river seems harmless, maybe the 2♣, your chances of winning this pot with a $10 bluff are essentially zero. Your opponent would be crazy to fold to a $10 bet with over $60 in the pot.

In a no-limit game I might be able to knock a player off pocket 10s. My bets could get intimidatingly large. And my opponent would have a tough decision if I played the hand as though I had pocket Kings. He'd have to consider whether he wanted to commit a lot of money with shaky cards when I seemed to think I had something a whole lot better. Moreover, as I showed in Philadelphia and Virginia, bluffs can be used to set an opponent up for a big fall. Once people saw me as a reckless bully, they were far more likely to make very bad, very expensive calls.

In limit, I can't force these kinds of mistakes. If someone thinks I'm a maniacal, bluffing nut case, it's only going to cost him a bet or two to call me down and see the true strength of my hand. If he's wrong and I do have a hand, it's no big deal. He's only lost a couple of bets. To continue to bluff under such circumstances would be foolhardy. I know I'd get called, and I'd be bleeding off money, one bet at a time.

Without bluffs, a profitable limit player—one who makes money over tens or hundreds of thousands of hands—is one who gets to his winning showdowns with the greatest efficiency. Every bet, call, fold, or raise is geared to that goal. He presses the smallest statistical advantages as hard as he can. If he feels he has a 51 percent advantage, he must raise, because over thousands of iterations, that is the most efficient, most profitable play. If he's behind, he'll call only if his chances of ending with the best hand compare favorably to the size of the pot. Any failure to raise, call, or fold in proper accordance with the math inevitably effects long-term profitability.

There are highly proscriptive guides to help players in their quest to play optimal limit hold 'em. *Hold 'Em Poker for Advanced Players,* considered by many to be the best limit hold 'em book on the market, contains a set of hand groupings. Group 1, for example, contains pocket Aces, pocket Kings, pocket Queens, pocket Jacks, and Ace-King suited. The authors, David Sklansky and Mason Malmuth, provide exact instruction on which groupings require which actions in which positions. It's a formula—and an effective one at that.

The programmatic nature of limit makes it perfect for online play. With most actions dictated by criteria that can be viewed at a glance—the cards, the size of the pot, the number of players in the hand—a good player can log on to a poker site and competently play multiple tables simultaneously. Online limit players can also use programs such as Poker Tracker to thoroughly analyze their play. After logging a statistically relevant number of hands, a limit player can get a pretty good idea of how well he's playing and what he needs to do to improve.

For a solid medium-stakes limit player, there's no compelling reason to play live. At a casino, a good dealer might distribute thirty-five hands in an hour. At that rate, over the long term a good limit player expects to earn 1 to 1.5 big bets per hour, depending on table conditions. So at a $15-$30 live game, $45 per hour would be a good take over the long haul. But online, it's common to see seventy hands an hour at one table. I know people who manage four tables simultaneously with earn rates approaching $200 per hour.

What surprises many is that the biggest cash games in the

world are limit, rather than some form of big bet. This is actually a concession to the fish. In a no-limit game, a good player can manipulate bets in ways that will ensure that bad players are making dreadful decisions. A novice will have almost no chance of leaving a no-limit game with money when surrounded by pros. When a fish realizes that he's thoroughly outclassed, he's likely to be humiliated, and he won't come back. In limit, though, there are no ruinous mistakes. A wealthy fish who sits with the top pros in a limit game will occasionally have winning nights. He may never realize that his few bad decisions a night make long-term profit impossible. He loses slowly—so slowly, in fact, that he may not notice that the experts are bleeding him dry.

Still, many big-bet players—myself included—consider limit a dry, mechanical exercise, one that lacks the psychological intrigue and excitement of no-limit. I think of limit as a form of competitive algebra, and I don't especially like algebra.

I, like most, came to poker with some misguided romanticism. From movies, I thought poker was a game of bluffs and rebluffs and monster calls with King-high. Though I've long since given up on the idea that poker is primarily a contest of wills, I've not resigned myself to a version of the game where courage plays no role. I'm competitive, and I want at least the opportunity to thoroughly destroy my opponents, to see their stricken faces when they realize that the previous hours' machinations were simply precursors to the one catastrophic hand that cost them every dollar they had in front of them.

Those moments provide a deep satisfaction that I could never experience in limit. I did not come to poker for the opportunity to grind away at the hapless for an hourly rate of one and a half big bets. That's just not why I play.

With no choices other than $15–$30 limit that twenty-fourth of December, I sat in on the first limit game I'd played in months.

I was doing my best to remember the Sklansky and Malmuth hand groupings (is King-Jack suited Group 2 or 3? And do I raise with Group 3 in middle position?) and trying to keep perfect track of my outs and odds. But I was getting distracted. I was being treated to a sort of Gulf Coast fashion show, and it was amazing.

A tall, trim man with a tight-fitting gray suit and cowboy boots sat to my right. His thick, gray hair started in a vertical ascent from the top of his head. After gaining a good two inches of altitude it swept back en masse. Along his temples, the hair pointed straight back, parallel to the floor. At the rear of his head the hair was parted precisely and feathered, making his entire hairdo a study in symmetry. It was a sculptural feat, achieved, I guessed, with a heavy-duty blow-dryer, a circular brush, and an astonishing quantity of hair-wrangling product.

Most of the other players sported two or three broad gold rings per hand, each decorated with some quantity of small diamonds. A few wore thick necklaces with large shiny pendants. Biloxi poker players love their bling.

In a couple of hours of play, I was pretty sure I made some errors. I failed to raise on the river with two-pair and made a needless river call. In the world of limit poker, making mistakes that cost two big bets in two hours is evidence of poor poker. But I still managed to scrape out a $60 win before the game broke around 6:30 P.M.

I couldn't bear the thought of playing a smaller game, so I left, praying a no-limit game would go on Christmas Day.


After a Christmas breakfast of watery coffee and a stale corn muffin, I headed back to the poker room. The no-limit game hadn't started, but it was looking promising; there were a few names on the waiting list, and I added my own. To kill the hour or two before we had enough players, I sat in on a $15-$30 game that was just starting.

The tone got nasty quickly. Andy, a jowly man with a felt hat and a leather jacket, berated a young man to his right after Andy's unimproved Ace-King lost to 4-5.

"You keep playing cards like that, I'll be sure to get you broke," Andy warned.

"You go right ahead," the younger man replied, sounding braver than he looked.

Initially, I was impressed by Andy's play. He was aggressive and tricky, unafraid to raise on a draw or take a stab at a pot. I thought it might be best to avoid confrontations with him. But over the next hour it seemed Andy was involved in nearly every big pot, and he attempted no fewer than three bluffs in that time. He clearly had some knowledge: He knew the value of a hand and spent some mental energy reading his opponents, but at nearly every opportunity he opted for the trickiest play possible. He raised on every draw and smooth-called on his made hands.

If Andy made the simplest available play on every street, he'd kill a loose game like this. But the fancy plays would destroy Andy's chances of profitability.

Once I recognized his predilections, I was able to steal a pot with 5-high from him because I knew Andy had missed his flush draw and wouldn't call my bet. In another hand, I check-raised Andy on both the flop and turn, which is as close to a bitch slap as one gets in poker.

When they called the list for the $5-$10 no-limit game, half the players at my table—Andy, and the worst of the rest—got up and headed to the game. I couldn't have been happier.

Within the first twenty hands I thought it might have been the best table I'd ever played. No draw was too distant, no flop too scary, for these folks. The pots were massive, and the most marginal hands were defended with mind-boggling calls. One player called off his entire stack with unimproved pocket 4s. My stack grew from $1,000 to $1,700 early when I hit a straight and wiped out a bewildered Texan who was incredulous that his two-pair was no good. Who'd figure you could lose with two-pair on a 9-T-J-8-4 board?

Soon after that, I was in middle position. Andy raised to $25, and an Asian man directly to his left raised to $50. The Texan whom I'd just wiped out flat-called the $50. I peeked at my cards and saw pocket Aces. With this cast of players I had no intention of being subtle. I wanted to announce my hand and clear the field, maybe get heads-up with the Asian guy.

"Two-fifty straight," I announced.

It was folded around to Andy, who looked at his cards, thought for a moment, then called. The Asian man also called. The flop was: Q♠-J♠-4♥.

This was not the flop I was looking for, as either of my opponents could reasonably hold pocket Jacks or Queens. Even Queen-Jack was a possibility with these two. And I didn't love my Aces much at all when Andy moved in for his remaining $400. I briefly considered folding, but then the Asian guy called off his remaining $300. Now a fold was out of the question. Against these opponents, there was a decent chance I was still ahead, and the pot was huge, over $1,500. So I called.

Andy showed Queen-Ten and the Asian guy Ace-Jack. I was way ahead. A ten on the turn gave Andy the pot.

I shook my head and managed to congratulate him. If he continued to play like this, he'd almost certainly leave broke. I might not be the one to get his money, but I'd have a shot.

Less than a half hour later, Andy played a massive pot with a mild-mannered Alabaman. After a series of bets and raises, Andy was all-in for about $1,700 on the turn. The players then turned over their cards. The Alabaman had pocket Kings, and Andy Ace-Jack. He'd missed both the flop and the turn and was clearly up against a better hand, yet he still called off every dollar in front of him. The river brought the miracle Ace.

Andy then stood up and screamed, "Skin it back to the fat meat!" Before the dealer could push him the pot, Andy was stalking the room, looking for acquaintances. He found someone in the $15-$30 game who'd listen, and he retold the hand as it happened.

"He bet $1,000 on the turn, and I called with Ace-high," Andy bragged. "Then that beautiful Ace hit on the river."

He then moved on to another player and retold the story, proudly announcing his willingness to throw all his money in the pot with three outs. I'd never seen a man so proud of his incompetence. The Alabaman, to his credit, said nothing, just reached into his pocket for more money.

Sadly, Andy didn't play another hand. He put his pile of chips into racks and headed for the exit. But even after he left, there were enough fish to make the game immensely profitable.

The session didn't proceed well. I flopped a set of 5s—a great hand against weak competition—but had to surrender a sizeable pot when the river brought a fourth heart and I faced a large bet. Shortly thereafter, while holding pocket Queens, I looked at a board of K-9-9-Q. I had Queens full of 9s—a monster. And I lost $1,000 to quad 9s. The table let out a collective gasp after seeing these hands.

The man to my right then remarked, "Boy, you are snakebit."

"You shouldn't be driving today with your luck," another offered.

They were right, I thought. This wasn't my day, and I was determined to learn from my experience at the Taj. If I stayed, I risked tilting. And I was not going to do that again.

An hour later, after driving over ice-covered roads to my hotel, I found myself in bed trying without success to find something worth watching on the television. It was early and I was bored. I picked up Brunson's *Poker Wisdom of a Champion* and reread an essay about a proposition bet he failed to adequately explore. He'd have made a fortune if he'd taken the time to thoroughly examine the opportunity, but he failed to, and that cost him money.

I thought of my own mental state at the table. Was I tilting? No. I was fine. I was thinking clearly and hadn't made a bad decision yet that night. I was just stuck. Yet I left what might have been the best table I'd ever seen because I was worried that I might tilt. How much had the lost opportunity cost me? I'll never know.

Control. I simply had to learn self-control. I harkened back to the mantra Dr. Hermann suggested for me as I learned to control my tendency to respond to adversity with hysterical fits.

*"Work pragmatically with the situation. Deal only with what you can."* The simple ideas helped calm me after the burglary. Maybe they could help me control my demeanor at the table. I decided to give it a try during my next tough session.

I added a day to my stay in Biloxi in hopes of playing the no-limit game again. I stayed around the casino for hours, but the game didn't go. With the loss, my total profit for the trip was $2,700, a far cry from where I wanted to be.

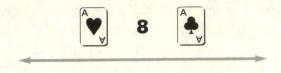

# NEW ORLEANS

**P**OPULAR DEPICTIONS OF POKER PLAYERS HIGHLIGHT THE sexier skills good players exhibit: bravery, intuition, ease under pressure, but movies, books, and television do a lousy job of depicting a talent that may be more important than any of these: endurance. Poker is a game that has a lot of dead time. Most players are involved in only about 30 percent of the hands dealt, and a sizable majority of these have quick, pro forma outcomes. You bet, some opponent folds, you take a small pot. Next hand. The signature confrontations—the ones that I talk about in the book, the ones that serve as turning points in movies—happen once every few hours, if that often. A good player has to find a way to stay interested through the long periods of nothingness—the interminable stretches of unplayable starting hands, the deathly slow dealers, and tablemates who agonize at length over the most mundane decisions.

About a year before I started my trip I went to Foxwoods to report on the $10,000 buy-in main event of the World Poker Finals, a World Poker Tour event. At about 12:30 A.M., after fourteen hours of play on the third day of the tournament, the field was down to the final ten. The last six would advance to the final day, which would be taped for the Travel Channel. There were several players of high repute at the table, Chris Bjorn, Brian Haveson, and Hoyt Corkins among them, but they all looked ready to keel over on their chips. Only one player remained focused, ready to battle. That was Phil Hellmuth Jr.

Hellmuth, winner of nine World Series bracelets, is a notorious figure in poker. The self-described "Poker Brat," he'll often berate an opponent or stalk the room cursing his luck after losing a hand. When he wins a pot, he'll shamelessly high-five friends on the rail; hours later, he'll berate a victor for showing no class after a far tamer celebration. During the 2004 World Series, while in a room with the best players in the world, he had the temerity to say, "I guess if it were all about skill, I'd win every one." His rants and tirades are a favorite of ESPN, and he seems to manage an embarrassing display for every broadcast.

His obnoxiousness has brought him a great deal of visibility, which he's ably parlayed into business opportunities. Through books, a syndicated newspaper column, and mass-marketed hand-held games, Hellmuth now makes his living by being Hellmuth. In 2004 and the first half of 2005, by his own admission, he played poorly and made most of his money away from the tables.

But that night at Foxwoods, one of his greatest poker skills was on display. At 1:30 A.M., he leaned forward into the table, his palms propping up his chin. His posture, his hand movements, his continual raises, communicated one clear message: I'm in charge here. Meanwhile his tablemates slouched against the backs of their chairs, listless and wary, and as Hellmuth attacked, no one found the energy to fight back. By the time they were down to the final six, Hellmuth had padded his already deep stack significantly.

Stamina was one of the most potent weapons Brunson, Moss, Preston, and many of the other all-time greats brought to the table. So many of their best anecdotes start with phrases like "We'd been playing for thirty-nine hours straight." Those were the moments when they were at their best. Or more to the point, that was when their depleted opposition was at its worst.

I've never been one for endlessly long sessions. After eight or nine hours my focus flags, a haze settles over my thinking, and I can't trust myself to make good decisions. Frequently I've left good tables because I could no longer play well. I know I've left some very profitable situations simply because I was tired. This was a major problem. I think that finding ways to play optimally for longer sessions might be the single most important thing I could do to improve my annual earnings. I should probably eat better, work out more frequently, and give up on caffeine and the little alcohol I drink. That would help, but living as a professional gambler while practicing the habits of a vegan is more contradiction than I can bear.

I might be inclined to play longer sessions if I didn't find the aesthetics of poker trying. In New York, for example, before the poker boom there was only one live action spot in town. It was on Fourteenth Street, just a couple of blocks west of Union Square, on the second floor of a nondescript low-rent office building. The space itself was clean enough, and the redundant security cameras and multiple doors imparted a feeling of safety. But the manager was a tyrant who spoke at all times in an enraged bark. Dealers, patrons—it didn't matter who he was speaking to or what the situation was—he was yelling. "This table three?" I once asked. "That's table eight! Table three is in the back!" he bellowed, veins protruding above his thick brown eyebrows. Another time, while playing a tournament in the winter, I was at a table where half the people were wearing parkas—it was that cold. We asked if they could turn off the ventilation fan that was piping in frigid outdoor air. Mike turned livid. The fan would remain on, we were told. Anyone who argued would be tossed from the club.

Even if Mike was in a decent mood, Fourteenth Street presented a legion of annoyances. The Gypsies were cheating. Persian Steve, one of the best and easily the most aggressive player in the area, was continually jawing, berating others for playing a pussy brand of poker. Robert, one of the dealers who looked like a fifties-era palooka, was among the dumbest, most incompetent people I've seen in any profession. It seemed every third hand was a misdeal. The club's biggest fish, a fiftyish restaurateur named Alfredo, was usually screaming. The walking stereotype of a New York Italian, Alfredo had a thick head of mostly gray hair, a wide chest, and a round belly. Everything about his posture and demeanor seemed to say, "Go fuck yourself." If he won after donating huge amounts of money with a trash hand, he'd triumphantly scream, "Buddy, it's all in the flop!" But usually he'd lose and start on a curse-laden diatribe against whoever happened to be raking his chips. "I fuckin' raise and you play that fuckin' shit!" he said to me in a venomous tone one evening after I had relieved him of $800 on a hand. An hour later he was still cursing in my ear. But Alfredo was tolerable because he lost huge sums of money. Some guessed that in the course of a year he had given away well over $100,000.

Lenny, another of the club's regulars, had no such redeeming virtues. A short, round man with closely cropped blond hair, he hosted an unimaginable set of odors. When I was in his presence, the distinct smell of some food—usually peanut butter or banana— would meet my senses first. Those mellow, welcomed aromas would invite lungs to fully experience the available air. Only when inhalation was at its deepest would the densely pungent and sickly sweet body odor reveal itself. It came in a rush—an attack—flooding the synapses in the same way that a burst of agony does. It was the olfactory equivalent of a baseball bat to the face. And Lenny was a rock, an absolute nonfactor at the table. He gave no action and he got no action. At times it seemed his only purpose in life was to provide a unique type of misery to those around him.

Shortly after my trip, the Fourteenth Street club and another uptown club were raided and shut down by the police. For many in the New York poker world, it was a loss. I didn't much care. There were other places around the city to play.


Even with Fourteenth Street as my training ground, I'd never experienced a spot as grating as Harrah's New Orleans. The casino, located at the foot of Canal Street directly across from the Riverwalk, was nice enough, decorated with a Mardi Gras theme. Like most casinos, the majority of the floor space was taken by slots—ringing, clanking, buzzing slots. In Harrah's, only a short fence and a narrow walkway separated the poker room from a massive slot bank. When I sat into the $5-$5 no-limit hold 'em game—the biggest game they spread—I was shocked that my seat was just inches from the rail, and only six or seven feet from the closest slots.

The slot noises—the warbling electronic bleeps, the coin-on-aluminum clanks—were incessant and grating. Initial attempts at friendly conversation with tablemates floundered; it was too much work above the din. Even the public address system used to call poker players to their seats had to fight over the slot noise. Speakers seemed to be directly behind every seat I chose. "John, three-six hold 'em . . ." Clank-clank. Ring-ring-ring. "John . . . last call for John . . ." A migraine never seemed far off.

I tracked down the poker room manager and suggested that he do what every other casino in the world does—move their biggest game to the room's quietest spot. He told me that they kept it there because of the location's visibility; he thought the game provided an inducement for those walking by. I didn't see the point in arguing, but I wondered whether the image of ten stonily silent, miserable card players was a great advertisement for much of anything.

My first day in New Orleans, the players were frighteningly tough. They were very tight and very aggressive. The pots were tiny. I knew I'd be in New Orleans for a few days, so I left, thinking I'd return when the conditions were more profitable. Next time I'd bring earplugs.

One of the great regrets of my life is that I've lost touch with wonderful people. In every place I've lived, I've made great friends. When I moved on, I rarely made the effort needed to maintain the friendship. At times, when I allow myself to think about my laziness in this regard and what it's cost me, I feel profoundly sad. In college, I thought that my platonic friend Bonnie and I got along so well that we might be well suited for marriage. I haven't spoken to her in more than a decade.

There is a notable exception: Mary Frances, another platonic friend, who happened to be my prom date. We've remained close, and she is without question my oldest friend. At the time of my trip, prior to Hurricane Katrina, she lived in New Orleans with her husband, Everett. An hour after my first session of poker, I sat with Mary at the kitchen table in her charming house admiring her corgi and telling stories.

"Look at this," she said, pointing to a clear plastic plate with a cartoon of a little girl painted in the middle. In bold pink letters above the girl were the words: "FOR A GREAT SISTER." It was a bizarre piece of kitsch, an appropriate gift for a six- or seven-year-old girl.

"It's lovely," I said.

She laughed and placed the plate on the accompanying pink plastic pedestal that held it upright. "An old blues singer that Everett sometimes plays with gave us this for Christmas. He's really the sweetest man. But I don't think he can read."

We laughed. Everett came in about that time and I asked how one might classify such an item.

"I think the general term for such things," Everett offered in an authoritative bass tone, "is keepsake."

I couldn't keep myself from laughing hysterically.

Mary and Everett both work as crew in New Orleans's active

film industry and he plays blues guitar brilliantly in a variety of bands around town. Their jobs and avocations are littered with more freakish characters than even a poker-playing New Yorker might hope to encounter. For the next few hours I listened to their stories about these characters: a stoned-out gold-toothed rap artist so cheap that he brought in his hibachi-toting father to provide lunch for the forty-person crew shooting his video; an insufferably pretentious art director who used a single name, wore a boa, and referred to herself in the third person; an obsequious and officious teamster who, for no reason anyone could understand, was shortchanging his workers so that an L.A.-based production company would save a few bucks.

A beer, some TV after dinner, and a comfortable bed. I slept better that night than I had in the month I'd been on the road.

In the morning I woke well after Mary and Everett had gone to work. I propped myself up and immediately saw Elmore, Mary's brown Welsh corgi, who had been sitting patiently by my bed waiting for a sign of consciousness. I made eye contact and his tail began to wag. He let out a mighty bark.

"Morning, Elmore. How about we go for a walk and get some coffee?"

On that beautiful, sunny morning, it seemed like a splendid idea to both of us.


I went back to Harrah's later that day and settled in to the right of Rick, a fortyish Louisianan with a ragged T-shirt and a head of thick, wiry salt-and-pepper hair. Rick was a minor celebrity here. It seemed every dealer and half the players knew him by name. When an acquaintance came by, he offered an immediate update on his session. "Up a thousand-twenty-five," he'd say without a question being asked. As he played, he kept meticulous track of his growing stack.

As he took down a few hands, he grew increasingly confident. He caught me bluffing on a hand where most players would have folded. He was in the midst of his ministreak, and the pot left him far too proud of himself. "Up a thousand-four-hundred," he announced to the next guy who ambled by. The man gave a dispassionate nod.

Erik Seidel, the great tournament player, once said to me, "Sometimes you can hear two words from a guy's mouth and know he's drawing dead for life." Rick was one of these guys. After he said, "I have to go in just a couple of minutes," for the fifth time, I knew he'd leave broke—that he always leaves broke. He'd press his wins, play too aggressively, and eventually run into a big hand. It was bound to happen. I could only hope that I'd be the one holding the big hand when Rick imploded.

A little while later I was in the big blind, and Rick opted to "straddle." When a player straddles, he puts out what is in effect a third blind that is double the size of the big blind. Posting a straddle gives the player the option of acting last preflop, even after the big blind has acted. Generally, straddling is a stupid move. Early-position play in hold 'em—either from the blinds or the positions just to the left of them—is difficult under the best of circumstances. When the rest of the field gets to see what early players do, they can react accordingly. For this reason, most players are very circumspect when playing in early position.

Straddling can be fun and add some juice to a dead game, but it's rarely a good strategic move.

As soon as he straddled, I knew Rick was going to raise when it got to him, no matter what two cards he held. He was too cocky at the moment. He couldn't resist.

In one of those moments when the poker God's gifts seem infinitely great, I looked at my cards and saw two red Aces. There were two limpers to me, and I had to decide how to play it. Normally, I'd put in a healthy raise in this spot—make my opponents pay to see a flop, and maybe get one of the limpers to fold. But if I made a standard raise to something like $35, I was likely to be called by Rick and the two other players, who'd be hoping to hit the flop and win a big pot. Out of position against three opponents, pocket Aces is a very tough hand to play.

With Rick sitting eagerly on his straddle, I made an unconventional decision: I checked—opted not to raise. Then, just as I expected, Rick raised to $25. After the two limpers called the raise, I made a ridiculously large reraise: $250 straight. A more appropriate raise would have been something like $150, but I thought Rick would call this overbet, suspecting I was bluffing again, and the others would fold. Rick's chips were in the pot instantly, and the other two players bailed out.

The flop was: Q♣-5♦-5♥

This was about as good a flop as I could hope for, and I announced, "All-in." Rick called in an instant and turned over a Q♦-T♦. Nine hundred of his hard-won profit was headed to my stack when he didn't improve on the turn and the river. The malicious pride that accompanies such a thrashing welled within me as Rick was forced to reach into his stack and count out enough chips to match my all-in bet.

I was hopeful that more might come my way. Rick had another four hundred, and he was likely on a little bit of tilt. I intensified my focus, hopeful that I'd be the one to complete the gutting of this fish.

Alas, someone else got the remainder of Rick's stack. At that point, the games got brutally tough. I was moved to another table where, in the three seat, there sat a chain-smoking bald man with a grim demeanor who accumulated a pile of ash on the felt in front of him. Other players called him "Professor"—he teaches at LSU—and my initial impression was that he was very tight and very tough. Evan, the man in the seven seat, had a long poker history. He had managed one of the rooms in Biloxi, and though he was evasive when I asked, I was pretty sure he was a pro. Four others were disciplined and cautious. In the next three hours we essentially traded blinds; someone would raise, everyone else would fold. We were all staying out of trouble, not wanting to make mistakes against a group that would effectively exploit errors. There was one big pot, but it was an unavoidable collision. One very big hand ran into a slightly bigger hand.

It was the first time on this trip, and maybe the first time in a year, that I'd sat at a table with no clear idea of how I could make money. I didn't see any leaks. I didn't see any hints of fishiness. So I didn't stay long. I'd do better searching out a game online with some decent action.

My no-limit hold 'em education followed a well-trod path. First I learned the virtue of patience. Play tight, wait for a first-class hand, and play it strong: This is what all the books preach. When playing few hands, opponents tended to give me credit when I entered a pot raising. If they wanted to call and play postflop, they were on the defensive. Even if I played a hand like Ace-King and missed the flop, a bet would often be enough to win because opponents were inclined to give me leeway; even if they were unsure, it was usually safest to avoid confrontation.

When opponents were ready to believe I held quality cards, it was reasonably easy to get a sense of their holdings. If I raised with pocket Jacks against someone trained to show me deference and I faced a reraise, I'd have to think I was up against a better pair, or at a minimum, Ace-King. My caution made others cautious; thus their indications of strength could be taken at face value.

In the early stages, I also learned the true value of starting cards: pocket Aces and pocket Kings are great, but everything else should be handled with care. Pocket Queens will run into Kings and Aces more often than you'd expect, and you'd rather not go broke when you're in that sad circumstance. As T. J. Cloutier said in *Championship No-Limit and Pot-Limit Hold'em,* if you can't get away from Queens preflop, you have no business playing no-limit hold 'em. Further, I learned to view Ace-Queen and Ace-Jack as trash hands whose primary purpose was to get me broke. I, like nearly every other decent player, learned the hard way that if you see action with Ace-Jack, you're almost always up against a better hand. On a Jack-high flop you go broke against Kings, on an Ace-high flop you go broke against Ace-King.

After some time, I also learned the sad reality of pocket Aces. As the poker axiom goes, "Aces will win you a small pot or lose you a big one." Aces get outflopped more frequently than you'd expect, and on those occasions when an opponent hits two-pair or a set, it's so difficult to fold those beautiful cards that were once so dominant and come around only once every 221 deals.

Eventually I came to see that the greatest profit could be made from toppling a hand like Aces or Ace-King. By starting with a low or medium pocket pair and calling a raise preflop I stood to make a fortune if a matching third card hit on the flop. When that set appears, it doesn't take a whole lot of work to capture an opponent's entire stack.

With the former lessons firmly ingrained, I came to treat any single pair—even Aces—with caution. It's a good hand, but I could be patient and wait for something better, maybe a set, before committing all of my money.

But sets don't come around that frequently. A pocket pair will appear once every 17 deals and a set will come on the flop only once for every 8.5 pocket pairs dealt. So a player will see a set once in every 144 hands; at a casino, that's about once every four hours. And on those occasions there's no guarantee that the set will make you any money; sets lose to flushes and straights, and they also come when opponents have missed the flop entirely, so you win an insubstantial sum.

The ultratight phase didn't last long. I found I was capable of patience, but didn't have the disposition to endure that sort of tedium. So I searched for ways to take advantage of those playing as cautious as I had been. I knew a tight, intermediate-level player doesn't like playing large pots without a near lock and can be bluffed and forced into uncomfortable decisions. When I spotted one of these players, I badgered him with bets and raises and stole pots that were rightly his. With a little luck my apparent recklessness might force that player into a horrible decision at a vital moment.

I also grew to see value in playing the middle of the deck. Most books will tell you to stay away from a hand like 8♦-7♦, but I found that if I raised with it and hit a flop, I stood to win a large pot.

As I played in New Orleans the day before New Year's, this was my level of sophistication. I could beat the loose beginners, the type I'd seen at the casinos in Foxwoods, Atlantic City, and Biloxi. Against them my weapon was patience; I could wait for a hand. I could destroy the intermediates, the type I'd encountered in Philadelphia, Virginia, and Atlanta. I knew how to turn their discretion against them by stealing pots and manifesting tilt.

As I looked around the table on my next venture to Harrah's in New Orleans, I saw none of the familiar flaws. Most of the tough players from my previous session had returned. These guys clearly knew the value of a hand, but beyond that, I didn't think they'd be especially impressed by tiltboy behavior. Some raises of $50 or $100 weren't about to force this crew into $1,000 mistakes. Plus, they were deep. The $1,500 I had in front of me gave me a very average stack. At this table I was among the least comfortable with the stakes.

I searched for less egregious, more individualized flaws. The cigarette-smoking Professor liked to know where he stood on a hand—he wasn't much of a gambler—but he was far from weak. Forcing him off a hand would probably require bets on multiple streets and cost most of my stack. I wasn't sure I had that in me, even if the opportunity presented itself.

Evan was also there, and I thought I had spotted a legitimate leak in his game—a bit of stubbornness on something like top pair, decent kicker. It was a fascinating problem, because Evan was an excellent player who knew how to value a hand, yet he'd give away money on those notoriously troublesome hands, like Ace-Queen and Ace-Jack.

While on the button, I was dealt Ace-King. There were three limpers to me, and I raised to $35. Evan called, as did two of the limpers. The flop was A-6-2, perfect for me. It was checked to me and I bet $125. Evan called and the other players folded. The turn brought a 9, leaving no possibility of a straight or flush. Evan checked to me and I had to decide on a course of action. The pot had nearly $400 in it, so my bet would be in the neighborhood of $300. My intermediate's instincts told me to avoid a big pot against a good player with only one pair.

I checked.

The river was a 7. Evan checked and rather than bet, I showed my hand. He nodded and tossed his cards in the muck. He must have had A-T or A-J. I was ahead, way ahead, and though at some level I knew it, I didn't have the nerve to bet my hand. I didn't have the confidence to exploit the one leak I'd spotted at the table.

After another hour I announced to anyone who would listen, "This game sucks." There was no argument. The Professor told me that with New Year's just a day away, it was worth sticking around. The Sugar Bowl was at the Superdome, and the teams, Auburn and Virginia Tech, would be accompanied by hordes of heavy gambling tourists. The action, he said, would be great. There'd be some fish for the rest of us to split up.

New Orleans locals didn't head to Bourbon Street on New Year's Eve. Instead they went to a stretch of Orleans Street away from downtown where a wide grassy median separated the two directions of traffic. Starting at about 10:00 P.M., people from surrounding houses dragged their dead and tinder-dry Christmas trees there and piled them high. Gasoline was added. A crowd gathered with most toting small arsenals of fireworks. By 11:00, firecrackers exploded by the thousands, while more sophisticated items shot skyward and detonated in colorful but less-than-thrilling displays. The air filled with smoke. At about ten minutes to midnight someone tired of waiting for the proper moment and threw a match on the trees. Twenty-foot-high flames cast a beautiful light and impressive heat. The fire department didn't bother showing up for a while, and even then they stayed in their trucks and waved to onlookers as if this was just another Mardi Gras parade.

It's possible that I attended the very last bonfire of this sort. After Katrina and the floods, there's no way to know what the texture of this neighborhood will be in the coming years, but if this tradition is rekindled, I'll happily attend.

The games at Harrah's never improved. My remaining sessions there were short. I got in extensive football time with Mary and Everett and ate the best garlic and oyster po'boy imaginable. Elmore and I became great friends.

I'd managed a slim profit in New Orleans, bringing my total profit to just more than $3,000. My bankroll stood at $18,200.

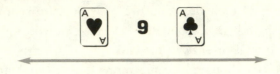

# TUNICA

ROUTE 61 STRETCHES FROM BATON ROUGE, LOUISIANA, through the westernmost portions of Mississippi and ends in Memphis, Tennessee. Off 61, there are long fields of cotton and signs pointing to antebellum estates. It's beautiful, historic country, a reminder of the land's agrarian past and the region's former source of wealth. Mechanized farming destroyed the profitability of cotton in such areas long ago, and for decades western Mississippi was among the most destitute regions in the country. By some estimates, in the 1980s the single poorest county in the country was Tunica, Mississippi, about twenty-five miles south of Memphis. In the late 1980s the 9,000 residents of the county suffered a 26 percent unemployment rate, with an average household income of under $12,000.

The 1990 law that allowed the Gulf Coast to legalize casino gambling opened the same possibility in Tunica County, and its residents quickly approved the industry. Gambling entrepreneurs took small steps at first, as Tunica was considered by most to be too out-of-the-way to be a thriving gambling town. By 1992, riverboats were operating, and they were wildly successful. The first casinos followed, and the patrons came to fill them. Tunica's fortunate proximity to the 1.2 million residents of Memphis and the heavily traveled I-40 freeway made it an instant success. As additional casinos opened, the reach of Tunica's popularity expanded. It turned out that Tunica was the most convenient gambling destination for a good portion of the country. For most of the South, nearly all of the Midwest, and a significant portion of the Plains states, Tunica was either a short drive or a short flight away. Sure, there were riverboats along the Mississippi in many states, but they didn't have the comfortable, cheap hotels, the huge variety of slots and table games, or the multi-course buffets.

Gambling has been good to Tunica. The casinos employ nearly 16,000 in a county where the population hovers around 10,000. Welfare and food stamp rolls are way down. The roads in the area are smooth and wide, and word is that the schools are some of the best funded in the state.

There is nothing to do in Tunica—no scenic spots, no shows or culture of any kind. The people who travel to Tunica know this. They go intending to gamble and gamble hard. The casino operators, aware of their customers' mind-sets, built their marketing messages accordingly. The repeating "on-hold" message at the Horseshoe Casino at the time of my visit boasted, "While many casinos in Vegas are geared toward the family, we cater to adults. . . . You won't find any pirate ships or roller coasters here." It's all about gambling in Tunica.

As I walked through the Horseshoe just after arrival, there were no distractions, no opulence or neon or anything else that might keep me from the sole purpose of my presence there. Somehow the setting got to me—and quickly. Within an hour I was playing way over my head.

I arrived in Tunica on the Tuesday following New Year's Day, which was two days before the events of the World Poker Open (part of the World Poker Tour) would commence. The hotels hosting the four weeks of tournaments and side action—the Horseshoe and the adjacent Gold Strike—were still largely empty and quiet.

I wandered into the small poker room at Horseshoe looking for a hold 'em game, but the only no-limit game they had going that night had a long waiting list. It looked like it might be a couple of hours before I got a seat. But the floor man told me that there was a seat in the $5-$10-$25 pot-limit Omaha game. I took one look and declined the seat. Around the table, most of the players had stacks of $100 bills in front of them. Two of the players had in excess of $5,000 on the table, and one thin sixty-year-old with dyed black hair and a tracksuit had what I estimated to be $10,000 or $15,000 stacked on the felt.

This game was simply too big for me. I didn't have nearly the bankroll to play multithousand-dollar pots a couple of times an hour. And even if I did, my Omaha game wasn't all that sharp.

Omaha is similar in structure to hold 'em; the only real difference is that players are dealt four hole cards instead of two at the start of each hand. Then there's betting, a flop, a turn, and a river—just like in hold 'em. But at showdown, players must use exactly two of their hole cards when constructing their best five-card poker hand. The two extra hole cards radically change the math of the game and the type of hands that are typically shown down. Thus winning strategies are quite different.

For example, in hold 'em, if a player holds aces preflop, he knows that against any single opponent he's always a 4-to-1 favorite or better; against a hand like Ace-King, he'll win more than 90 percent of the time. In Omaha, even the best possible starting hand, something like A♦-A♣-T♦-J♣, is only a 3-to-2 favorite over 4♦-5♣-6♥-7♣. And with so many cards in play in Omaha, hands develop where one player, having flopped the nuts, is actually not a favorite to win, because another player holds a powerful multi-way draw.

If, for instance, one player held K♥-Q♦-6♥-5♦ and the flop came 9♠-T♠-J♦, that player would have the nut straight—9-T-J-Q-K—the best possible hand. But against a hand like J♠-A♠-J♣-Q♥, where the opponent holds full house and flush and higher straight draws, the straight isn't a favorite at all; it's exactly 50–50. You can be pretty sure on that flop that everyone's money is headed into the pot and luck will determine the winner.

After watching the game for about twenty minutes, I was mesmerized. Chips were ignored completely as hundred-dollar bills were counted and thrown by the fistful into mounds at the center of the table. After a showdown, a pile of bills was pushed to one player and the rest would congratulate him. Everyone, both the winners and all but one of the losers, seemed to be having a great time. It was Tunica, after all, and they were gambling. Gambling is fun.

Without even asking the floor man, I grabbed the nearest open seat and pealed fifteen hundreds off my roll. I immediately realized that I'm such an Omaha novice that I didn't know how to rate many of my starting hands. Most starting foursomes seemed to simultaneously embody characteristics of both hope and ruin. K♣-J♠-9♠-2♥? The high cards looked tempting and the flush draw offered promise, but I knew that a Jack-high flush was more likely to break a player than win him a big pot, as that Ace-high flush could very well be out there.

And by the time the betting reached me, there was almost always a raise. It would cost me either $100 or $125 to play. That seemed like a lot of money just to attempt to catch a flop.

Gaylon, the man two seats to my left, was responsible for a good deal of the raising. He was a mountain of a man, with a vast gut and forearms the size of my thighs. A pair of mirrored sunglasses sat atop his head, and a broad mustache descended from his lip to his chin, dominating his face. Gaylon raised nearly every pot, and if he didn't win the pot right there, he usually picked it up with a pot-sized bet on the flop. He had almost $10,000 in front of him after a couple of wins, and he was doing a pretty good job of running over the table.

About twenty minutes into the session I was in late position, holding 7♥-8♣-T♦-A♥. This, I thought, was a pretty good Omaha hand. (I've since learned that this is not the case.) There were straight possibilities and a nut flush draw. I called the $25. Gaylon, to no one's surprise, raised to $125 from the small blind. One other player called and I decided for once to see a flop.

The flop was 5♣-6♥-J♠.

My feeling at the time was that this is about as ugly an Omaha flop as exists—no flush draw, no ace, no king. There was really only one draw on the board—a straight draw, and I had it with my 7-8.

Gaylon bet out $400. The player between us folded. I thought that Gaylon would bet at this pot whether he hit it or not. He was a bully; and he'd use his stack, his aggressiveness, and his comfort with the stakes to run over me. I looked at the board again—5♣-6♥-J♠—and I couldn't imagine he connected with it. He was bluffing; I was sure of it.

I picked up my thin stack of bills and said, "$1,200." I counted out twelve bills, and Gaylon cocked his head, stunned.

"Wow," he said.

Oh, shit, I thought. He has to think about this. He has something.

"How long you been in town?" Gaylon asked.

I didn't respond.

"'Cause if you just got in to town, you wouldn't be doing that without the nuts."

Wrong.

He then pulled two 6s from his hole cards, placed them on the table for all to see, and folded. "Kills me to fold this," he said. He had a set of 6s, the second-best possible hand, and mucked it.

The table was stunned.

"Well, he wouldn't bet like that with nothing," Gaylon announced to the table, sounding defensive.

"What did you have?" asked an Asian man across the table. I shook my head, mostly because I was too astonished to speak.

In the next half hour I squandered the $800 I made in the hand against Gaylon by trying to see a few flops. I was out of my depth here. Even if my Omaha chops were sharp, my bankroll couldn't handle the kind of fluctuations I'd see in a game this size. When my hold 'em seat opened, I happily moved.

The best pot–limit Omaha players are known to love gambling. This may sound obvious. But in fact we're not all gamblers. In the world of poker, there are many players who despise gambling and some who adore it.

To better explain this unintuitive concept, I'll need to ignore the definition of "gambling" that one might glean from a dictionary. Instead, I'll need to describe how more advanced poker players go about determining the proper play in certain circumstances. For example, consider a hand of $5-$10 no–limit Texas hold 'em being contested by two players. One player holds A♠-T♠, and after the dealer places the river card on the table, the board is 6♠-7♠-J♦-A♣-2♥. This player was hoping to see a spade on the river, a card that would give him the nuts. But having missed that, he holds top pair, mediocre kicker. The other player in the hand bet aggressively on the flop and the turn, representing a fairly big hand, probably something like two-pair. On the river the aggressor in the hand bets $500 into a $600 pot, leaving the player having a lone pair of aces with a difficult decision.

How does this player determine the best course? He has to apply some simple math to the situation, using his intuition, experience, and history with the opponent to assign real values to the variables in the equation. In this situation it will cost the player $500 to win $1,100, so he's getting just better than 2 to 1 on his money. The other player has been representing two-pair, and there's no reason to ever put money in a pot when it's sure to go elsewhere. But there's something about the way the hand was played that makes the guy with Aces think that his adversary might have been bluffing, that he was betting some massive draw like 8♠-9♠ and missed both his flush and straight draws. Maybe it was a strange-sized bet on an earlier street, maybe it was a physical tell as the guy put out his large river bet. Whatever the indication was, some suspicion of a bluff has been raised.

Now the player with Aces has to determine the likelihood that he's facing a bluff. After lengthy consideration, he determines that there's a 60 percent chance that the other guy hit two-pair; there's roughly a 40 percent chance that he's looking at a bluff. Given this determination, the player ought to call the river bet. He's decided that he'll win this pot one in every 2.5 times it's played. To make the play profitable in the long term the call needs to be correct one in every three times it's played. Calling the bet, therefore, is the play with the highest expectation.

This calculation may seem dry and unambiguous, but in fact one's determination of the proper play in a spot like this has a lot to do with one's willingness to gamble. At best, a situation like this has a slim margin for profitability. There are any number of no-limit players who have no interest in putting in large sums when there's a good chance that they're losing. They'd rather wait to play a big pot when they are sure they are ahead. Moreover, a player's willingness to gamble will affect his approach to the calculation. A nongambler might decide that his opponent would bluff here only 20 percent of the time, whereas an avid gambler might suspect a bluff 80 percent of the time and call eagerly. A nongambler sees a sure loser and a gambler sees a clear winner.

A good pot-limit Omaha player is one who is willing to put his money into a number of pots where the outcome is far less than certain. Because of the statistical parity that often develops between made hands and big draws, the winning player at pot-limit Omaha has to enjoy gambling—tossing cash into pots where he knows he's likely to lose. He must be able to endure (indeed, enjoy) the fluctuations that accompany such situations.

I've heard top pros describe Lyle Berman and Robert Williamson III, perhaps the world's two greatest PLO players, as extraordinary gamblers. "He just doesn't give a shit," one pro said of Williamson. "He'll throw his money in on any four pieces of crap. That's why he's so dangerous."

I clearly had some willingness to gamble. I don't think anyone would describe me as a rock. In fact, I played a hand during my next session in Tunica that might have shown some incaution—a willingness to gamble a bit too much.

On my second day in Tunica, players eager for the World Poker Tour tournaments started arriving in droves. They came from all over the South, Midwest, and Prairie states. Again I was amazed by some Southern gamblers' sense of fashion. At a low-limit stud game sat a man with a long black ponytail that descended from his massive black cowboy hat. He wore mirrored sunglasses, had a full beard, and his black Western shirt had poker hands sewn into the lapels. When he stood he revealed a great belly that pulled at the gaps between the shirt's buttons. His skintight Wranglers revealed more contours than I wished to see. Every finger, save his thumbs, was adorned with a wide diamond-studded ring.

At my $2-$5 no-limit hold 'em table that night, a variety of America's regions were represented. To my left was an Oklahoman with slicked-back hair, a perfect shave, and a pierced ear. If he hadn't talked incessantly about his beloved Sooners—who were taking a beating at the hands of USC in the Rose Bowl, which we were all watching live—I would have pegged him as an urbanite. He would fit right into the Village, I thought, at some gay bar. He was a loquacious man. When he wasn't spouting Sooner-relevant statistics, he was recounting the same bad beat the entire table had heard many times.

"So we playing head's-up, and he raised . . ."

"We've already heard this," the Missourian to my right complained.

Sooner fan paused. "I reraised but he thought I was just trying to make a move—"

"I know. We all know. I don't want to hear this again."

Sooner fan stopped for a full thirty seconds. But he couldn't contain himself and finally blurted with ridiculous speed, "He thought I was just making a move so he went all in and I called, but he only had seven-deuce and he hit his two-pair on the river."

The Missourian shook his head.

The pots in this game were unusually big. In a $2-$5 game, buy-ins are normally capped at $500, but at this table there was no max buy-in, and several players, myself included, kept over $1,000 on the table. It seemed everyone was caught in a tough decision or two before long. So despite the mostly amiable chat, there was a tension, an edge in the air.

My own tough spot came quickly. I lost $700 early when I flopped top set on a board of 5-6-7—I had pocket 7s. I lost to a flopped straight. At that point, I decided to take a walk and get some dinner, hoping that when I returned the endless stream of cold decks I'd been encountering for the last month would finally come to an end.

After grazing at the thoroughly repulsive buffet at the Gold Strike, I returned to the table, where the mood seemed to have lightened. A fascinating and lively conversation was under way.

"I'm not saying there are no poor Jews," the might-be-gay Sooner fan said. "I'm just saying I've never met one." I couldn't imagine what drew the conversation to this subject.

"Ain't that the truth," the dealer chimed in, smiling.

A previously mute Texan suddenly brightened and added, "When Jewish people raise their kids, they make sure to teach them the Golden Rule: Buy low, sell high." Most at the table chuckled.

I sat silently, wondering if anyone would take notice of my larger-than-average nose or comparatively swarthy skin. No one did, and the conversation quickly turned back to the Rose Bowl, where the Sooners were being humiliated. I took a minute to digest the slightly shocking conversation. Jews are good with money, they thought, and from the best I could tell, they considered this an admirable cultural trait. There was no venom in anyone's tone. No one got near an epithet or statement that could be considered hateful. I smiled. Poker players might be culturally ignorant, but, for the most part, they were nice people.

The cards ran cold for a few hours and players were starting to comment that I was "tight as a drum." If this was my reputation, I figured, I might as well try to use it to my advantage, so when I saw 5♥-6♥ in middle position, I decided to open for a raise to $30. The player to my left—a legitimately tough opponent—and the big blind, a young man with bad teeth, a *Matrix*-style overcoat, and a greatly exaggerated sense of his ability, called.

The flop was A♣-9♦-4♠. I missed completely. But I decided to follow up my preflop aggression and attempt to take this pot down with a $90 bet. Essentially, I was saying to my opponents, "I have Ace-King. Get out! You've said I'm tight, so what the hell else could I be betting with?" But the message didn't get through. The player to my left made what I thought was a defiant call. There was some force in the way he put his chips forward, as if he wanted me to know he had a piece of this—that he did not intend to fold. Yet, I thought, the hand caused him some concern. I figured Ace-Jack.

The turn was the 5♦, giving me bottom pair. Now I was in as strange a predicament as I could recall encountering in my poker career. I was clearly behind in this hand—way behind—but I did not want to give up on the pot. First off, I thought there was a reasonable chance that my opponent would fold to a decent-sized bet. Moreover, if he did call, I had outs. If I hit a 5 or a 6 on the river, I'd have the winning hand. I desperately wanted to gamble here, to give myself a chance to hit a card. If I managed to spike my card and my opponent remained stubborn, there was a chance I'd get every dollar in front of my adversary. I took a few seconds to think: Was there a bet that could both induce a fold and, failing that, leave me decent odds if I was called and hit one of my cards on the river? I decided to bet $200, and he quickly called.

The river brought the stunning 5♣. "All-in," I announced. He called in an instant. He showed A-Q and I raked in a nearly $2,000 pot.

The man needing dental work then whistled and said, "God, you played that bad." I shrugged. It was a strange hand, no doubt, and would provide my somewhat poorer tablemate with a good bad-beat story. But there was logic to each of my actions—debatable logic, but logic nonetheless. And while this hand might have looked like a series of misplays that were bailed out by a stunning turn of luck, it could have been the most sophisticated hand I'd ever played. At the very least, it showed a willingness to gamble.

Dumb luck? Good play? Both? I thought about David St. Hubbins observation in *This Is Spinal Tap* that there's a fine line between clever and stupid.

The next day the Gold Strike opened a huge function room that was filled with oval poker tables. At one end, a dry-erase board listed a series of mouthwatering cash games—Omaha, hold 'em, triple-draw, stud. Most of the games were way beyond my bankroll, and I could see piles of cash at a couple of pot-limit Omaha tables. Toward the back, in the middle of the room, a man at a lectern placed players in satellites for the $500 no-limit hold 'em event that would start the next day. The line from the lectern made two right-angle turns before it snaked out of the room and into the hallway. There must have been 250 people in the line.

But I wasn't planning on playing that tournament. In fact, I was taking a few days off. Marisa was flying to Memphis, and we'd spend the weekend in the city, away from the poker tables.

The $500 buy-in no-limit tournament drew 1,449 of my peers. First place paid an almost surreal $174,663.

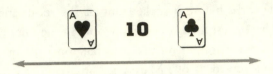

# TUNICA, PART II

EVERY YEAR MILLIONS OF PEOPLE WITH ESSENTIALLY NO interest in fine arts wind their way between guidebook-highlighted items at the Louvre, the Metropolitan Museum of Art, and the Prado, to name just a few notable institutions. I think most who take these journeys are hopeful they'll be entertained by what they see, but will be neither surprised nor disappointed if the works fail to stimulate a more profound appreciation. They go to these spots because it's what one does when traveling in Paris or New York or Madrid. If they don't like it so much, that's fine. At least they can answer in the affirmative when asked if they'd been there.

It was with similar motivations that Marisa and I made our way from Memphis International Airport directly to Graceland, former home of Elvis Presley, the King. The cost of the mansion tour, $20—nearly double the suggested donation at New York's Metropolitan Museum—was a shock. But we had no intention of bypassing this landmark, even though there was a driving rain and 34-degree temperatures that day.

At first we enjoyed the carpeted ceilings and zebra-patterned upholstery; we thought of it as an excellent permanent exhibit of seventies kitsch. As we wandered away from the main house and through the outlying buildings, we grew weary. The tour was slow, and many of the displays were underwhelming. (Did I really need to see the King's canceled checks?) After leaving a display of latter-day Elvis costumes, which included some glorious rhinestone-studded capes, we trotted through the pounding rain and Marisa commented, "I'm saturated." I was as well—and glad we hadn't bought the $27 Platinum Tour Package, as neither of us had the energy for the Automobile Museum or the self-guided airplane tour.

We were exhausted, she from working till 3:00 the previous night, me from playing till a similar hour. We devised a simple plan for the remainder of the afternoon: Check into our hotel and take a nap. An hour later, we were sound asleep in each other's arms.

Over the next two days we went to a Memphis Grizzlies NBA game, heard blues on Beale Street, ate Memphis's famed dry-barbecued ribs, and perused the Civil Rights Museum. In between the sights, we took ample time to admire each other, giggling, holding hands, and placing open palms on ready waists. It was a delight and a reminder of just how much joy and satisfaction Marisa and I derive from sharing our common interests. We love food and culture and sports and seeing new cities and sights.

It further reminded me that the frequent travel and bizarre hours I kept over the previous two years had prevented me from accompanying her on outings I would have enjoyed far more than a night of cards. If I were to leave poker and take an editorial job or move back to technology, I could certainly craft a schedule that would allow us to spend far more time together.

Sunday we had a drawn-out but tearless departure at the Memphis airport. She was New York-bound and I was heading back to Tunica. I so badly wanted to get on that plane.


In 2002, the single greatest development in the history of poker occurred: the creation of the World Poker Tour. Conceived as a series of high buy-in tournaments that would attract the world's best players, the action from the final tables was taped for television and broadcast in a series of two-hour events on the Travel Channel. Prior to the WPT, there was some poker on TV; ESPN annually broadcast a poorly produced hour-long compendium of highlights from the World Series of Poker's main event. But the WPT adopted a feature from the UK show, *Late Night Poker*: hole-card cameras. Viewers of the WPT could see what players held as the action developed. For the first time in the United States, poker fans could fully appreciate the drama and skill inherent in top-flight poker. It made for great reality TV.

The WPT quickly became the highest-rated show in the history of the Travel Channel. Before long, it spawned a series of imitators. Within two years no-limit hold 'em tournaments were on ESPN (*WSOP*), Fox Sports (*Poker Superstars*), The Game Show Network (*Poker Royale*), and Bravo (*Celebrity Poker Showdown*). ESPN's *WSOP* coverage expanded to include nine events, and their main event coverage ballooned to eight hours.

The WPT and its imitators brought hundreds of thousands of players and billions of dollars into the greater poker economy. It seemed every home-game hero who'd ever booked a $50 win saw a poker show and thought, "Hey, I can do that." Tournament fields swelled. In the inaugural event of the WPT, the 2002 World Poker Finals at Foxwoods, 89 players entered the $10,000 buy-in main event. In 2005, 674 played in the same tournament. In 2002, 639 played in the main event of WSOP. In 2005, 5,619 created a prize pool of $52,818,610, with the winner, Joseph Hachem, taking $7.5 million back to Australia for first place.

For poker tournament specialists, the influx of players was an unprecedented boon. Most novices came to these tournaments without nearly the skill or experience to compete effectively and had little shot at leaving with a significant share of the winnings. With all the dead money available, a fortunate tournament player could become a millionaire after a few days of work. In 2004, 22 players had tournament winnings of over $1 million, and 48 grossed over $500,000.

Getting through large fields requires an astounding amount of good fortune. One bad beat or one cold deck is usually all it takes to get eliminated from a tournament. And the larger the field, the greater the chances of a disastrous confrontation. Even the best tournament players know they might go a very long time without having a substantial payday. The fields are so large and the amount of luck needed is so great that Erik Seidel, one of the very best tournament players in the world, says that a year is no longer a sufficient period of time to judge one's results. You need to look at your results over a three- or even five-year period to really have a good idea of how you're doing, Seidel said. He noted that in 2004 he spent $250,000 in tournament entry fees alone, so a long dry spell could be painful, indeed.

"I'm competitive, and all the losing is tough," Lee Watkinson said to me after one tournament. This was shortly after a stretch in which Lee had two second-place finishes in major tournaments that netted him over $1 million. And if Watkinson was having a tough time, imagine how Phil Hellmuth Jr. and Scotty Nguyen must have felt. Both former world champions, they went through 2004 grossing less than $70,000 each.

No one can attest to the vicissitudes of tournament poker like Chip Jett. Jett started his poker career just after high school while working as a lifeguard at a pool near his Phoenix home. He thought that, like his uncle, he'd become a bartender. When Indian casinos opened in the area, he found himself drawn to the poker room. Every time he could scrape up $50, he made his way to the casino for some low-limit games. He got to know the dealers and heard that they were making about $25 an hour, far more than his lifeguard gig paid. So he enrolled in dealer school.

Before long he was a shift boss, and soon after that he became a "proposition player." (A proposition player receives a salary from a card room to play in games. They help casinos keep games running during nonpeak hours.) He did well in cash games, and after a couple of years he was playing in the biggest games that could be found in Arizona—as high as $40-$80 and $75-$150.

Soon he found that his truest gifts lay in tournaments. He played the $50 rebuy tournaments that were available in Phoenix. In one remarkable stretch in 1999 he made twenty-one final tables in twenty-four events. He liked the way tournaments defined his day. "When I played cash games, I wanted to stay at the table when I was losing," he said. "But with tournaments there was closure. When I lost, the day was done."

Then, in February 2001, he decided to test his skill on the greater poker scene. He went to Los Angeles to participate in every event of the Los Angeles Poker Classic at Commerce. He was unknown when he arrived, but not when he left. His results were so strong, in fact, that he won the Best All-Around Player Award for the LAPC. His picture was on the cover of *Poker Digest*. "That was validating," he said. "It was something I could show my parents."

He went on the tour full-time after that, playing in as many as 300 events in a year. In 2002 in Tunica, he met Karina, another poker pro. They spent time together over that year's World Series. At the close of WSOP events, after knowing each other for six months, the two were married.

As well as things were going, Jett had yet to score a huge win. "Incredibly unfortunate things would happen," Jett said. "I was remarkably unlucky in life-changing situations. I'd be in a huge pot that would give me a great chance at winning, then the guy would hit a one-outer. But I knew that if I kept putting myself in those situations, I was ready for a big year." Indeed. In 2003, Jett made several final tables, won more than $500,000, and won Phil Hellmuth's Champion of the Year Award. If not for one disastrously unlucky hand while playing heads-up against Howard Lederer in the Party Poker Million tournament, Jett would likely have won another $110,000.

But in 2004, when tournament fields ballooned, Jett did poorly. For the year he made only $52,654 in tournament prizes. He said ruefully, "If I had the kind of year in 2004 that I had in 2003, I'd have retired."

Still, he's philosophical. "You have to be thick-skinned," he said. "Most days when you go to work, you're going to get zero. You're going home empty-handed 70 to 80 percent of the time. . . . If you're the kind of person who needs to see progress every day, tournament poker is not the right spot for you."

He remains confident of his skill and believes that the large tournament fields and huge prize pools will one day benefit him greatly. But he admits that the tournament lifestyle is trying at times. Tournament poker requires near-constant travel. The schedule is so demanding that Lee Watkinson didn't have a home at the time I met him. There was no point; he spent all his time in hotels anyway. Jett is a homebody. He and Karina had a daughter and there's nothing he enjoys more than taking care of his little girl and fiddling with tools in his workshop. He's hopeful that one day in the not-too-distant future he'll crack one of the big tournaments. Then he'll be able to cut back significantly.

Even in the midst of his losing streak, Jett sounded upbeat and unburdened by the losing and the nomadic existence. "I'm adaptable," said Jett. "Whatever I need to do, I do it."


I don't believe I have the constitution to endure a stretch like the one Jett had in 2004. The months-long downswings that I encountered in cash games were tough on my psyche. My sanity and drive would suffer during a losing streak that lasted, say, two years. But even as a cash-game specialist, where the income was relatively stable, I couldn't fully escape the lifestyle that Jett, Watkinson, and Seidel endured. I'd have to travel. I'd have to leave Marisa and New York and go to Tunica and L.A. and

Vegas—that's where the good games are. That's where I'd find the highest concentration of fish.

If I ever needed evidence of the necessity of such travel, all I had to do was look at the sign-up board on display at the Gold Strike when I arrived back in Tunica. The board listed five $5-$10 no-limit hold 'em games, and a few pot-limit hold 'em games as well. Plus there was Omaha—no fewer than nine $5-$10 pot-limit Omaha tables.

And there were fish. In the first table I sat into, there was a man who seemed intent on illustrating the importance of my trip. He was around forty-five and had a large belly and a melanin-free complexion. Throughout the session he wore the strangest expression, as if he were at once uninterested in the game and completely overwhelmed by it. He'd call massive bets with any pair, and play any Ace from any position. I was card hot that afternoon, catching flops, and this guy simply couldn't fold a hand. Before long, after playing a rather unadventurous brand of poker, I was up $3,000, my best session of the trip.


"Hey, how you doing?"

"Good. We played together . . . on the Party Poker cruise?"

"No, I didn't play that one."

"Aruba?"

"Yeah, yeah. Right. You cash in on that one?"

"Nah."

"That was fun, though."

"Yeah. Great. Well . . . good luck."

Having spent so much time around poker the previous eighteen months, I was beginning to recognize many of the other players. I'd share a table with someone and we'd chat or maybe play an interesting hand together. But we shared no distinct memories, developed no affections. In fact, as I looked across the field of tables, I realized that I had no real friends in the place. While people I encountered were pleasant enough, I was lonely. The feeling was probably a reaction to the time spent with Marisa. Having seen her so recently, I was now acutely aware of her absence. After another few days in Tunica I started to get a little testy. My tablemates were getting on my nerves.

A couple of days after I returned, I was involved in another profitable session of $5-$10 pot-limit. I was playing aggressively, using a big stack and a hot run of cards to bully the table. I was picking up a number of small pots and having fun. Then I found K♦-Q♦ in the cutoff (the seat to the right of the button). It was folded to me and I raised to $40. The small blind called. I'd played with the small blind a few days earlier, and quickly developed an opinion of his style: He was tight—solid. When he played, he had a hand. Plus he was a little nasty. I remembered that he'd given a dealer an unnecessary chiding after a routine error.

The flop came: 8♣-Q♦-4♠. Perfect. I had top pair, good kicker. When the small blind checked to me, I bet the full size of the pot, $90. The small blind then paused and thought. I studied him during this delay but couldn't determine if his quandary was tied to the strength or the weakness of his hand. Was he slow-playing or thinking of folding? I couldn't tell. He called.

The turn was great for me: K♣. I now had top two-pair.

The small blind checked and I bet $200. Once again he gave some deep thought before calling. Then the river brought the A♥, making a board of 8♣-Q♦-4♠-K♣-A♥.

The small blind glanced up at me and said, "Well, you're going to put me all-in anyway, so I might as well do it myself." He pushed his remaining $500 into the pot. Disgusted, I shook my head. What kind of idiot did this guy think I was? If he had A-Q, I was beaten by his top two-pair; if he was drawing to the straight with T-J, he got there. If he was slow-playing a set of 8s, I was dead from the beginning. His gratuitous minispeech infuriated me.

"Oh, fuck you," I said in a soft voice as I threw my cards in the muck.

"What?"

"Nothing. Sorry." I decided it was time to end the session.

The next day started on a far more pleasant note. "Now, don't you come round here flashin' a big roll like you're going to scare somebody," said a man with an endearing Texas drawl as I sat down to his left. I looked at his round, smiling face, then at the pile of bills in front of him—there must have been $12,000—and laughed. Neither the roll that I flashed, about $3,000, nor the amount I peeled off it, $1,500, was about to scare anyone at that $5-$10-$25 pot-limit Omaha table. He chuckled along with me. His name, I learned, was Lloyd. And Lloyd played poker, though his real talent lay in poker commentary.

"I won most of this," he said, pointing to his stack. "You should have been here earlier. There was this guy, he'd call anything."

"Calling stations," I said. "Gotta love 'em."

"He'd call a squirrel out of a tree."

"Really?"

"He'd call a cat off a shrimp boat."

Lloyd enjoyed having me for an audience, as I was laughing at everything he said. After a few unpredictable turns in the conversation, he started talking about the poker club in Dallas that he ran. He gave me a card and I told him he'd definitely see me soon, as Dallas was my next stop.

"There's a guy in my club in Dallas," he said. "This guy could be a world-class gin rummy player. He has got a photographic memory. Can remember every card in the deck. Now, I also have a photographic memory. I just don't have any film."

I could not repress my giggle. Lloyd then gave me some background on his club, which he told me was where Byron "Cowboy" Wolford and other Texas greats used to play. I was hoping to take in more of Lloyd's stories, but he got up for a lunch break and soon after that the hold 'em seat I was waiting for came open. I despaired slightly, but I had Lloyd's card, and I planned on a long stay in Dallas, which is said to have the best underground poker scene in the country.

At my hold 'em table, I found another Texan, but this one was not nearly as affable. He was a tiny man—five feet four, rail thin, with a pointy, weasel-like face and a high-pitched nasal tone. "I'm here for your money," he announced, after plopping about $1,000 on the table.

Within ten minutes I got a good idea of how he played, and I was unimpressed. He called raises with just about any two cards, with the hope of cracking a big hand. It's a strategy that works for some heavy-action players, those unafraid to bluff frequently or continually pressure their opponents. Such a player gets value from bluffs and from getting paid off when he hits his two-pair. But this guy simply folded if he didn't hit. He'd bleed money $30 or $50 at a time over the course of the afternoon, I thought. Within an hour, though, he managed to win a $1,500 pot after cracking another player's Aces. But the feat was somewhat tarnished by the fact that he put all his money in as a big underdog. He flopped top pair, ended up all-in on the flop, then nailed trips on the turn.

"You better watch out," he said. "I got chips now."

"Yeah, we're terrified," I grunted, my tone speaking what I thought of both his play and his banter.

"I'm gonna help you get broke," he threatened.

"Like I said, I'm terrified."

"I played in Vegas against Johnny Moss," he informed me. "He didn't like playing against me, I tell you."

I rolled my eyes. Moss was perhaps the greatest poker player who ever lived. He made millions, and won most of that against the game's other greats. I couldn't imagine Moss giving this idiot a moment's thought.

"I played against Moss at the Sahara," another man at the table interjected. This guy was of a similar age, maybe sixty, and he was a rock. In the course of two hours he played only two hands, and he played those with a look of absolute terror on his face. Soon the two were arguing over who Johnny Moss had paid the higher compliments to.

Johnny Moss died in 1997, before I started playing poker seriously, yet evidence of his skills was sitting right in front of me. He had managed to convince two fish—one a chip bleeder, one an ossified stone—that they had world-class talent. Sparse compliments he'd paid them three decades prior to our game in Tunica was enough to keep these two donating for a good portion of their lives. Thank you, Mr. Moss. Thank you very much.

I found pocket Kings in the small blind a short while later. The weasel had limped, as had a player in late position. I raised to $50. Both players called. The flop was J♦-7♣-9♥, a good flop for Kings. I didn't screw around. I bet $150.

"That's a defensive bet," said the weasel. I didn't understand the point of his comment—was he saying that I missed the flop or that I was protecting my overpair while playing out of position? Whatever. If he wanted to raise, I'd push him all-in, especially after that comment. I stared blankly at him. After a not-so-dramatic pause, he threw his cards in the muck.

At the end of the day I'd netted another thousand and was up just more than $4,500 for my time in Tunica.

With two days left in Tunica, I decided to put some money and energy toward winning a seat in a $1,000 buy-in no-limit hold 'em tournament. I arrived in the poker room early, signed up for the first $100 satellite they offered, and I won it. With the whole day before me, I moved back to the cash games feeling confident. My luck, it seemed, had finally turned and I was now, as the poker players say, "running good."

The table that morning was typical of what I'd seen in Tunica—a mix of ages, geographic origins, and skill levels, including a few fish. I'd do well, I was sure of it. But the session started out poorly. On a hand early in the session I raised with K♦-K♥ preflop and was called in two spots. Then, on a flop of 7♣-8♣-9♠, I bet $100, and was immediately raised to $350 by the only player at the table wearing a cowboy hat. Then, to my shock, the fish in the hand flat-called the $350. My Kings might have been best at that moment. I could have been up against a flush draw and a straight draw. But this was more action than I wanted with one pair. I unceremoniously folded. The original raiser took down the pot with a set of 8s; the fish went broke on the turn, calling an all-in with his flush draw.

No problem, I thought, pocket Kings lose all the time, and I made the correct, albeit easy, laydown. Later I raised with Ace-King, hit an Ace on the flop, and was immediately faced with a huge reraise from a very weak player. It was the first raise I'd witnessed from him and decided he wouldn't do this with anything less than two-pair. When I folded, he was obliging enough to confirm that my read was right. Some twenty minutes later, I was in the big blind with A♠-4♠. I usually wouldn't play this hand, but an early position raise was called by three people. It cost me only $30 and there was $150 in the pot. The A♦-7♣-4♦ flop gave me two-pair. I checked, figuring someone else had an Ace worth betting. A late position player obliged with a $75 bet, which I immediately raised to $350. He called and everyone else folded.

The turn was the 7♦, which rendered my hand worthless. If my opponent had a flush draw, he hit; if he had an Ace with a better kicker, I was now behind. Hell, if he had a 7, I was crushed. The truth was that I didn't mind this card too much. If something like the 2♦ hit instead, I couldn't be sure if I was against a flush or an Ace with a good kicker. I'd probably put a fair amount of money in the pot while drawing very slim. But with this card,

I knew I was done. I had only one choice, check-fold. I showed my hand to the table before throwing it in the muck.

At this point, I was starting to get sympathy from my compatriots. "You're snakebit today," said a genial Southerner across the table—the second time I'd heard that phrase on the trip. I nodded, and reminded myself that, yes, I was stuck, but I was playing well. I lost about as little as I could on some very tough cards.

The wear must have been showing on my face. Twice more I had to lay down big hands, and both times my sympathetic competition showed me their superior cards. One young man, a competent Missourian with a bookish face, said, "I'm showing you this because I respect your game." A fish gave me a similar courtesy and said, "I'm sorry it had to be you." I told him I shared the sentiment.

As tough as things were going, though, I wasn't going to leave the table. There was money to be made here, and I was playing decently. I didn't think I was tilting, and I didn't want to make the mistake I'd made in Biloxi, leaving a table simply because I was stuck. I was controlling what I could. I was fine.

Happily, I had a distraction from my miseries. At the adjacent table, the biggest game east of Vegas was under way: $50-$100, pot-limit Omaha. The average stack was well over $10,000, with some having as much as $50,000 in play, most of it in bound piles of $100s. At various points in the day, recognizable pros circulated through the game. Josh Arieh, a twenty-something tournament specialist who finished third in the 2004 World Series, made a very strange-looking $12,000 bluff that was caught by two players. Freedy Deeb played briefly, and "Eskimo" Clark sat in for an hour.

The undeniable star at the game was Dave "Devilfish" Ulliot, a flamboyant Brit with thin, slicked-backed brown hair. The previous times I'd seen Devilfish—at a bar in Vegas, in a poker hall in Aruba—he had reveled in the attention and adulation a WPT win had brought him. He liked being a celebrity. At the bar in Vegas he joked loudly with his companions, and in Aruba, apropos of nothing, he sat down at a long-unused piano and began plugging away at a tune. He wasn't very good, but everyone turned to see who was playing.

That day his spirits were far lower. He was stuck, hemorrhaging money. In one hand he was heads-up with a young player who couldn't have been more than twenty-five. (How he got the kind of cash needed to play in that game was anyone's guess.) From what I could see, the kid looked intimidated by the stakes. Most of his actions were hesitant; his brow furrowed with concern. Yet, on a board that contained three spades, Devilfish called bets on the turn and the river that totaled about $15,000. The kid showed both the Ace and the King of spades. I was stunned. Even Omaha novices know that drawing to a flush without the Ace of that suit will often lead to disaster. But in this case Devilfish lacked not only the Ace of spades, but the King as well. What the hell could he have? Would he call those bets with two-pair or a set?

"You have the Queen-high flush?" the kid asked as he raked in the mass of bills and chips. Devilfish grimaced.

Later, Devilfish won back a large portion of his money when he hit a two-outer. When I saw his cards, 3-3-T-6, I wondered why he would bother playing them at all. While I don't think I'm necessarily capable of judging a player of Devilfish's accomplishments, I was pretty sure that at that moment he was playing horribly. Maybe losing $50,000 put him on a bit of a tilt.

Back at my table, I found myself in the first favorable spot I'd encountered in hours. I had called a raise with J♦-T♦ and hit the flop hard: J♥-T♠-3♣. When the preflop raiser, the bookish Missourian, bet $100, I raised to $400, and he reluctantly called. I welcomed his money in the pot, as I was clearly ahead.

Then the turn: 3♦. Damn. If he had an overpair—pocket Aces or Kings—he now had a better two-pair, and my hand was a loser. He checked, and I checked behind him. The river brought the 6♣, and he bet out $500.

"Fuck. Every fucking hand tonight," I whined.

I still had top two-pair, a very good hand considering the board. I was ahead of everything but a big pair. I called. He showed Aces.

I left the table then, having lost $3,000 of the $4,500 I'd won in Tunica, $900 of it on that final hand. As I fumed and ruminated in my hotel room an hour later, I concluded that I didn't need to lose the final $500. I was beat, and at some level I knew it. But I'd seen too many tough hands that day, made too many laydowns. When this key hand developed, I was exhausted, defeated. I no longer had the strength to make the proper, more difficult play. So in trying to compensate for my squeamishness from Biloxi, I overcompensated. I stayed at the table too long, past the point where I was capable of playing good poker. Despite my efforts, I appeared to be making very little progress on my issues of self-control.

I was sickened by the loss, my largest single-session bleeding of the trip. I wanted out of Tunica and no longer wanted to play in the tournament I'd won into. I asked the staff if I could have the $1,000 entry fee returned to me. But they weren't obliging. I'd need to get permission from the tournament director, and he wasn't available.

After a night's sleep I felt calmer and decided to play in the tournament. I played well, I think, but it went as most tournaments go. After four hours of heavy concentration and deft play I ended up busting out on a hand I could play no other way. Ten minutes later I was in my car, looking for the nearest crossing of the Mississippi River.

My bankroll stood at $19,000.

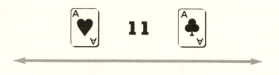

# DALLAS

**I**N TUNICA EVERY THIRD PERSON I SAT NEXT TO WAS IN ONE way or another involved with a poker club in Dallas. They were dealers, managers, co-owners—everyone had a spot to promote. By the time I left Tunica, I had accumulated enough numbers and business cards to keep me busy for several days. Beyond those contacts, I had an acquaintance from the area, Dan, who seemed eager to show me around the Dallas poker scene. Dan, like me, was making a living by playing poker and writing about the game.

When I informed Dan of my impending arrival via cell phone while a half day away, he got to work. By the time I checked into my hotel that Saturday afternoon, I had a half dozen e-mails from Dan, each with information on a club I could go to that night. Look them over, he suggested, and pick one. He'd make the necessary calls to ensure I was allowed entrance. One of the notices looked especially interesting: a grand opening north of the city. The e-mail advertised a $2,000 freeroll that would be followed by a variety of games: everything from $1-$2 no-limit to $25-$50 pot limit. Sounded exciting.

I phoned to ask for directions and was told it would be a twenty-minute drive from my hotel. ("Everything in Dallas is twenty minutes away," the locals say, though I can assure you that on this matter they are lying.) I easily doubled that time after getting lost amid a series of nondescript strip office complexes. I had to call the club three times while within a mile of the place, asking for some sort of recognizable landmark by which I could get some bearing. If he had initially told me it was two doors down from the Christian Fellowship Center, I would have found it a lot quicker.

The markings on the club's door were suitably vague: A small placard that read JBM Training was the only hint that the space was occupied. When I rang the buzzer, a respectable-looking sixtyish man who bore a resemblance to Dick Cheney, complete with suit and tie, welcomed me into an anteroom. I handed my driver's license to the Veep and filled out a form. In return I was given a laminated card that gave me a "lifetime membership" in this club.

I was then led through a rear door, which revealed the poker space. About forty people milled about, drinking beer and snacking on the provided enchiladas and quesadillas that were warmed in stainless steel, Sterno-heated serving dishes. As I entered, I saw that the tables were covered with gleaming slick green canvas and the chips had edges that had yet to be rounded by shuffling. The unmarred white walls were decorated with framed posters from gambling movies—*The Sting, Rounders, Casino*. A smoking space walled off by plexiglass covered the far wall, and to my right was a small "high-limit room." The chairs in that room had higher backs and appeared more luxurious, and the door to the room could be shut for privacy. By poker standards, the space was tasteful and spacious. The owners had put more effort into the decor than any underground room I'd seen.

"Hey, Jay," someone called. I wasn't expecting anyone to recognize me here, two thousand miles from home, but there was one of my Tunica tablemates, Matthew, a tall, dark twenty-two-year-old who was affiliated with another club that I was planning on seeing during my visit. In fact, I had a card with his number in my wallet. As we chatted about the great action in Tunica, a familiar-looking man of a similar age approached the two of us. He knew Matthew and eyed me questioningly. We'd met, and it only took us a few moments to recall where: Vegas earlier in the year. What was Stew up to? He was starting a club of his own, of course. He showed me his club's chips, which were very nice. But did Dallas really need yet another poker room? Stew thought there was plenty of opportunity remaining.

Soon we were called to our seats for the start of the freeroll, which was conducted with a festive energy. The young entrepreneur-managers of the club wore suits and dealt, as did their pretty girlfriends. None had any real skill or experience dealing, but their enthusiasm for their new venture was infectious. And as no one was risking any of his own money, errors were overlooked and the table chatter was lively and cheery. I busted out of the tournament quickly, and had to wait for a cash game. It took nearly an hour, but eventually a $2-$4 no-limit game started.

I bought in for the max, $400, as did one other player, but the other three at the table bought in for the minimum, $100. Coming off of Tunica, where I'd had as much as $4,000 in my stack, the dim prospects for action here were disappointing. Even if I won every dime available—a very unlikely outcome—I'd win well less than $1,000.

Once under way, the game was predictably torturous. The short-stacked players clung to their chips, refusing to offer even the minimal action their buy-ins allowed. As they waited for the perfect opportunity to commit, I grew restless.

"Any chance we'll get to break in that high-limit room to-night?" I asked one of the managers.

He shook his head. "Doubtful."

In fact, the young crowd that attended this opening was more comfortable with even lower stakes. When a $1-$2 no-limit table opened, everyone migrated there, and for lack of a better option, I did as well. For a half hour I played with total indifference to the money in front of me, raising frequently and calling on any sort of draw. Still I was bored and was readying to leave when Matthew tapped me on the shoulder.

"You want to play some pot-limit Omaha?" he asked.

"Absolutely." Even if the stakes were low, Omaha has action.

"They won't start a table for us here, but another guy here owns a club that will give us a table."

"We're going to Stew's club?"

"No, another guy has a club."

"OK. Um. How many people here own other clubs in the city? Are you all doing recon work?"

Matthew chuckled. A few minutes later we were heading for the parking lot. For a half hour, I followed the high taillights of Matthew's massive pickup through a series of interchanges and highways. Then we parked in a semi-industrial business park and walked to yet another unmarked door and entered yet another club.

The ensuing game was friendly and active. Pots were big for a $1-$2 game, and most of the players threw their chips into pots without a great deal of concern for the consequences. I hit a couple of cards and managed to leave up $500 for the night.


The first night in Dallas reminded me of how much I disliked freerolls, the entry-free tournaments clubs sometimes offer. Sure, the chance to win without any risk is appealing, but generally a freeroll is offered as an inducement to get players in, and once the tournament has started, the club's only goal is to end it as quickly as possible and get players into raked cash games. Freerolls usually have lightning-fast blind structures that remove most of the skill from the game. As a semipro, I'm better off paying into a tournament that gives me a chance at outplaying the competition.

Normally I avoid freerolls, but the one that Dan encouraged me to attend that Sunday sounded particularly interesting. It was at the Lodge. Modeled after a country hunting spot, maybe something one would find in Montana, the Lodge was decorated with most of the things you'd expect to find in a country hunting retreat: dark woods, deep fireplaces, rustic furniture, mounted animal heads, and, of course, poles that nearly naked women danced around. The Lodge is one of Dallas's many strip clubs. Apparently Sunday business was slow, so they asked Dan to run a weekly poker tournament.

The prizes were modest by any standard—gift certificates, topping out at $150 for first place. But this didn't keep people away. Five tables were full when I arrived, and the waiting list had thirty-six names. The structure Dan created was among the most generous I'd seen for any small tournament. The blinds started small and increased every twenty minutes. Dan told me the tournament could last as long as six hours. This was fine for the club: They wanted the players to pay for drinks and watch (and tip) some of the girls.

After arriving, Dan seated me at a packed octagonal table. Our dealer was a young woman, maybe twenty-one, with short blond hair parted to the side. Her white skin sagged a bit around her jawline. Still, she was attractive in the way that all young women are, though she was far from beautiful. With her red halter top, I thought she looked like Lisa Simpson might if she ever reached her early twenties.

Her dealing was awkward, and she made a series of mistakes I didn't feel the need to point out—it was a freeroll, after all. About fifteen minutes into the tournament, she announced, "Another five bucks and the boobs come out."

"I'll contribute to the areola fund," said the man to my left. He handed her a five-spot. Down went the halter top and out came the boobs. They were unspectacular, not large, not especially pert, but fine. If I were her boyfriend I'd enjoy them, I thought. The unrestrained breasts in no way hindered her dealing. More remarkably they had no noticeable impact on the play.

Freeroll or no, breasts or no, the players were approaching the game with a fiery intensity. One player at my table wore dark sunglasses, which is silly enough in a freeroll, but the Lodge was dark—really dark. I often had to check my cards multiple times to determine the suits.

When I busted out, I sat at the bar waiting for a burger when another player sat down a couple of stools away and asked, "Bad beat?"

"There are no bad beats here," I replied. "It's a freeroll. Plus there's tits."

He shrugged, unwilling to agree.

After eating I went to the restroom, and the man at the adjacent urinal—a fellow with an unkempt beard and crooked teeth—started a conversation.

"I was here when they made that," he said, his eyes on a poster over the urinal. In the poster, an otherwise naked woman reposed on a velvet sheet, only playing cards—Aces—covered her breasts and groin. Some text on the poster told of the day and time of the tournament.

"They should have put the Ace of spades over her left titty," he offered. I looked, and noticed the Ace of diamonds on the left breast. It looked fine to me.

"You're quite the perfectionist," I replied.

"Huh?"

"Nothing."


Ask a poker player about his luck and you'll often be subjected to an aggrieved rant. Of course, serious players would never claim to be "unlucky," because everyone knows that poker over the long term is not about luck. Saying such a thing would seem ridiculous from a pro. Rather, the complaints get specific. *I never win a race. If I have a hand and there's a flush draw out there, it's going to hit. I haven't hit a set in three weeks.* By isolating aspects of the deck's cruel caprice, they remove laughable generality from the complaint. But really, the message is identical—*My luck sucks*—and everyone knows it.

If a player I respect tells me about such a run, where he's lost twelve races in a row or found his sets repeatedly beaten, I'd likely believe him. I've been there. I know these things happen. But even so, I have no sympathy for him. Over time I've become inured. I've heard the same shit so many times that I just don't care.

Yet when things are going badly for me, I catch myself saying the things I can't stand to hear. *"Every fucking hand!"* I screamed in Tunica after enduring hours of a desperate session. I said this as if I hadn't gone runner-runner to take a $2,500 pot two days earlier, as if I hadn't distributed two bad beats to win the only satellite I played. When I catch a lucky card or give a bad beat, I feel the forces of chance are providing only mild compensation for the horrors they have repeatedly rained upon me. *I deserved to go runner-runner for once in my life,* I think. *How many fucking times have I seen it go against me?*

This is the way poker players are. We unsmilingly skip over our good fortune and agonize over the bad. It makes us insufferable. We are narcissistic, so focused on our personal miseries that we're unable to get through a few moments of small talk or express an opinion without descending into bad-beat stories.

I realize we're not unique. Teachers and lawyers and people in all walks of life complain at their jobs and among their friends. But at least there is some individuality to their difficulties. Coworkers and clients and interpersonal dynamics vary, and learning the origins of someone else's stresses can be compelling. But one story of a five-outer sounds exactly like another. Further, if a friend describes, for example, an angry, unreasonable boss, I can listen to the story with the understanding that the situation was entirely unexpected and the resulting suffering completely underserved.

No poker player could make such a claim. We know exactly what we're getting into each time we're dealt a hand. Yet we can't shut up. And when I think about poker as a career, I cringe at the thought of decades' worth of bad-beat stories. Somewhere along the way, I'll have to find a way to endure my peers.

The evening following the strip joint tournament, Dan took me to the Apex Club, a warehouse-sized space with walls painted in bright red, green, yellow, and blue, sectioned like some giant kindergarten. There were only two tables going in the vast space, and Dan and I had to wait for a seat. Finally, when we had six interested people, we started a $2-$5 no-limit game. I bought in for the maximum, $500. Dan bought in for $300. Most of the other players bought in short as well.

Immediately I sensed how the game would proceed. I'd play like I had in Philadelphia and Atlanta and Greenville. I'd attack, I'd bluff, and, more likely than not, I'd win, but even if I lost, my bankroll wouldn't be substantially affected—a $500 win or a $300 loss just wasn't that big a deal to me. With the stacks so short, chances were that I wouldn't play a single hand that would be taxing or intense. If I suspected a bluff, I'd call: The $300 my opponents had wasn't enough to make me second-guess the advisability of any raise or call.

When my Ace-King cracked pocket Kings, I gave a simple shrug and raked the pot. When my top-pair–top kicker ran into a set, my response was equally impassive. I won a few hundred and left, bored.

I am an ambitious person. I've approached every hobby or profession with restlessness, an eagerness to improve. For instance, when I landed my first job as a technology writer, simply reporting wasn't enough for me. From almost the first day on the job I was looking to expand my responsibilities and knowledge. At times my efforts probably seemed ridiculous to my new colleagues, as I was recommending projects of dubious viability that I, of course, would lead. While nothing came of most of my ideas, my energy, my want of accomplishment, served me well. Only two years after entering the tech writing field, I was writing books and advising Fortune 100 companies on matters I was completely ignorant of just a couple of years earlier.

In poker, I started on a similarly determined path. From the very first days at Fourteenth Street, when I played $4-$8 limit, I looked over at the big game—the $5-$5 pot-limit—and thought that before long I'd be playing there. The players at that table would buy in for well over $1,000, sometimes as much as $3,000 or $4,000, and huge pots were the norm. The lineup was extraordinarily tough. Guy, an Australian who nearly won a World Series bracelet, was a regular, as was Tommy, a giant of a man with a long ponytail who many claimed was the best big-bet player in New York. Persian Steve, a dark, sharp-tongued man who forever wore a leather jacket and a scowl, served as a de facto emcee, offering continual raises and brutal critiques of others' play.

Midway through my trip, in light of how I had played in Dallas, I was forced to think once again about my need for achievement, my desire to prove my ability. Poker and ambition are a potentially dangerous mix. As a professional, I needed to find a way to stem my need to prove my comparative talents. A pro should have one goal when he enters a poker room: to make as much money as possible. By seeking challenges, by looking to best ever tougher competition, I was overlooking profitable opportunities. I know in the past I've walked by a table with several fish so that I could play in a game that I found more challenging and interesting.

A player with greater discipline, with a greater sense of his purpose, will drift to the most profitable seat without a thought of going elsewhere. I could learn from my friend Greg in this regard. Pride isn't a factor in his table selection. He'll play far lower stakes than his bankroll will allow if he determines that that is the best way to make money.

In Dallas it seemed clear that once I prove myself against a certain class of players, I lose interest in the games and get bored. If I wanted to be a pro who enjoyed success over a long time, I'd need to approach the medium-stakes game the way a middle manager goes about a day of work that has been nearly identical to the thousands that have preceded it. I needed to be an adult, a responsible breadwinner who did what was required of him.

I needed to give up on the sophomoric notion that I had to prove I was better than I was. Immaturity: yet another personality flaw I'd need to repair if I was going to make it in this game.

# 12

# AUSTIN AND HOUSTON

I DROVE TO AUSTIN WITH LOW EXPECTATIONS. THE DISTRICT attorney for the state's capital took a far greater interest in poker than his counterpart in Dallas and had shut down all the poker rooms that dared to open in his jurisdiction. From what I'd heard from a few people in the area, Austin hadn't housed a large club since 2003, when a high-profile bust shut down the city's only busy spot. But there was still hope, I thought. I was going to a small-stakes home game my first night, and somebody there might know of some solid local action—maybe a tougher-to-find, higher-stakes home game. Even if the scene was anemic, I still had plenty to look forward to. I loved Austin. In a couple of trips I'd made to the area in the preceding years, I'd come to adore its small but nifty downtown, its wonderful music scene, and the cheap, tasty food. Plus I had a friend in the area, Tim, whom I'd see the day after I arrived.

The first night, I drove from my hotel to a suburban apartment complex to play in the home game run by an area poker blogger. The crammed apartment was bustling, with as many as seven people waiting for a seat to open in the ten-person game. The game was tiny—50¢-$1.00 pot-limit—and the stakes couldn't hold my attention. But the players were from a demographic I hadn't encountered on my trip: They were young, smart professionals, most just out of college or grad school. Two had MIT undergrad degrees, and another a Harvard MBA. They worked in and around the city's vibrant high-tech industry, and from the sound of things, they were doing well.

In coming years, I thought, the members of this group might host their weekly games in the spacious rooms of their sprawling houses. Their salaries would inevitably rise, as would their positions in society. Their aging parents would crow about their impressive careers to anyone who would listen. I found the near-complete absence of observable dysfunction relieving. It served as a reminder that there were still people in this country pursuing lives of steady, predictable accomplishment. These were the people who could keep the economy and government functioning. Lord knows, the folks I was seeing at the poker table weren't up to the task.

Two of the players, including the host, Joshua, were engaged, and he was nice enough to share his copy of *The Complete Idiot's Guide to Being a Groom* with me. As I perused the first pages, I was reminded of how horribly negligent I had been. The book started with a very basic assumption: The engagement was set, and a ring sat upon the future bride's finger. Only then, it seemed, could one plan a wedding. I resolved to shop for and purchase a ring before I left Austin. Marisa and I had talked about doing the shopping together, but this would be a surprise she'd love.

I departed the game early, desiring a night's sleep that would leave me with a discerning eye in the morning. Still, I managed to drop $140, a fairly remarkable and slightly embarrassing feat at those stakes.

Early the next day, I entered the jewelry stores near my downtown hotel. I offered the bits of vocabulary I'd learned from my short New York ring-shopping experience. "A bezel setting," I said, echoing a desire Marisa had stated. But my words were met with disdain. Bezel settings, which fully surround a gem, occlude light and thus reduce the brilliance of fine diamonds, the salesmen said, and they didn't offer such settings. What they showed me looked sparkly enough but contravened Marisa's desire for an unpretentious ring that sat nearly flat on her finger. The roll of bills I'd taken with me for the shopping remained in my pocket. Maybe we'd do this together after all.

The remainder of the day was lovely. Tim, his three-year-old son Harry, and I drove to Llano, a small town an hour and a half west of the city so that I could return to Cooper's, home of the best barbecue I'd ever eaten. Prior to Harry's birth, Tim had led a peripatetic life, having tried to make a living as an entrepreneur and musician. During my trip he was working as a freelance writer. On the drive through the arid Texas landscape, as he admired his beautiful son asleep in his car seat, Tim and I talked about the difficulty of our professions. The irregular income from freelance writing was tough for a family, he said, and he was considering changes that would provide the stability appropriate for his new responsibilities. We agreed that gambling would not be a reasonable alternative career.

Cooper's, as I remembered, served the most succulent meats I'd ever tasted. The ribs, huge and fatty, were infused with a slightly vinegary marinade that enlivened taste buds across the palate. The London broil was perfectly cooked—red at the center—and wonderfully chewy and rich. We ate until we could barely move, and then managed only a short trip to a local park, where we spent an hour digesting as Harry played with his miniature earthmoving machinery.


That evening I made my way to another suburb of Austin to play in a $2-$5 no-limit game that I discovered through Joshua's game. When I found myself in a small apartment that was entirely undecorated, save for a poker table, TV, and small futon, I was disappointed. The two college-age men who were running the space sat on the floor engrossed in a PlayStation football game while I sat quietly on the futon, hoping other players would eventually arrive. After a half hour, it seemed clear I was the only one who'd show up. So I left and headed back to my hotel.

My hotel offered free wireless Internet, so I played that evening's session online. The cards treated me well. I won more than $2,000 in less than two hours.

During the trip, I'd played Internet poker intermittently, on days when I traveled or when live games were difficult to find. The contrast between live and Internet play I saw in these weeks reinforced an opinion I'd held for some time: In most places in the country—New York included—it is impossible to make as much money live as can be made online. This wasn't revolutionary wisdom or a break from widely held belief. Among serious medium-stakes players, one who doesn't log significant hours online is considered foolish. The games are too good to ignore.

Still, some very good players refuse to play online, and they offer a few reasons for their hesitance. The most commonly cited concerns involve the fairness of online play. Skeptical players point out that colluding players could use an instant messaging program like AIM to gain an advantage, primarily by exchanging information on hole cards. While this possibility exists—and I'm certain that it does happen—the fact is that colluders on the Internet are more likely to get caught than their live-game counterparts. Ray Bitar, the president of Tiltware, the software-development company behind FullTiltPoker.com, pointed out to me that the keepers of Internet poker sites have perfect information. If two players are working together to create action that hurts opponents, the keepers of the site can react to accusations of cheating. They can review unseen cards at a later time and learn the likely motivations of those involved. At a live casino, however, once a hand is dead and the cards are reshuffled in the deck, any suspicions will remain just that. There is no way to effectively investigate a claim of impropriety. Furthermore, Bitar noted that online sites can employ preemptive measures to catch colluders. For two players to work together effectively, they'll need to log thousands of hands at the same tables. Algorithms within the software can spot this tendency; those involved can be thoroughly investigated.

Some also worry about the integrity of the sites themselves and postulate that some of the players are actually computer-generated robots that are purposefully dealt advantageous cards. It's difficult to disprove such claims, but it's hard to believe that engaging in such practices would make fiscal sense for the poker sites. Party Poker had as many as 70,000 concurrent players contributing to raked hands at the time I wrote this book. They were doing so well that they had gone public with a $3 billion valuation. If an accusation of house robots or hand manipulations were ever proven, it's likely their user base would disappear and their profits along with it. It's hard to believe they or their competitors would engage in such practices.

The other major criticism of online play is that it is somehow a lesser form of poker. Some argue that without the ability to see your opponent's face and mannerisms it's impossible to pick up on critical tells in important situations. This claim is legitimate. There is clearly less information available from opponents who are represented by unflinching avatars.

But there are a couple of points that people who make this argument miss. First is that reading tells is a vastly overrated skill in poker, particularly at the middle stakes. At most tables I've played where the buy-ins are between $100 and $1,000, my opponents are capable of making huge mistakes at nearly every stage of a hand. They overvalue mediocre hands, they underbet their made hands, they play draws that are mathematically indefensible. In situations like these, tells have no bearing on the proper play: The math and the cards serve as the guides.

When tells come into play, there's usually something glaringly obvious—some abrupt change in my opponent's affect or behavior that I observed in a similar situation—that forces me toward an action. Other times when I consider tells, I'm facing a very close decision, where the cards and the math seem to make a variety of actions equally reasonable. Or I've interpreted a bet or a raise as being inappropriate for a situation. In those moments, I'm looking for some final nugget of information to steer me toward the best possible decision. But even in these cases, the actions—the bets and raises—are the primary consideration.

I have made some daring calls and huge laydowns based on physical information. Indeed, I feel I'm pretty good at picking up on these things. (What poker player doesn't feel he has a gift for this?) But I've also gone days without basing a single decision on any sort of specific tell.

No less an authority than Daniel Negreanu has discussed the relative lack of importance of tells. In a brilliant article in *Card Player* magazine, Negreanu stated that tell reading is not nearly as critical a skill as most think it is. Body language and physical actions are components used to fully analyze a situation, he said, but previous action and estimations of a player's abilities are far more vital in making quality decisions. This type of information is fully available online.

(An aside: In televised broadcasts in 2003 and 2004, Phil Hellmuth Jr. was seen making some amazing laydowns. At points it seemed that he was, as he claimed, looking into his opponents' souls, making phenomenal use of body language to escape from difficult situations. But those folds need to be viewed in a larger context. In tournaments, Hellmuth employs a well-documented strategy of avoiding big pots. He relentlessly attacks blinds and antes and attempts to build his stack without putting large portions of his chips at risk in any one hand. When met with significant resistance or shows of strength, Hellmuth errs on the side of caution. As one top pro said to me, "He [Hellmuth] was playing some scary weak poker." In fact, in several televised events, Hellmuth can be seen making very poor laydowns, folding hands that were prohibitive favorites. When the tendency became well known, Hellmuth was met with constant reraises. Another pro said to me, "Every schmo is now moving in on him, knowing that he'll fold pretty much anything.")

When playing on the Internet, any edge that I might lose by not having an opponent's face to scrutinize is more than compensated for by the speed with which hands are played. If I am more skilled than another player and I have only a limited time to play against him, I'd far prefer a hundred hands per hour without the benefit of tells than I would thirty hands per hour while looking directly at him. It's not even close.

Online play is viable enough to have created a new class of poker professional. Across the country and throughout the world, there are thousands of people who make their livings playing online. Though there's no way to properly estimate the number of online pros, there's no question that they outnumber live-game professionals by a significant margin.

One reason for this is that the barrier for entry is much lower online. Any player with a modest bankroll, say $1,200, and a solid intermediate's grasp of limit hold 'em can make upward of $30 per hour online while playing four simultaneous tables of $2–$4 limit. To make a similar sum live, a player needs a bankroll of about $6,000 and will have to endure downswings of at least $2,000 while playing $15–$30. When I got out of college, I didn't make anywhere near $30 per hour.

Of the group of aspiring players I met on the Upper East Side in 2002, three are now full-time pros who almost never play live. Two of them are limit specialists, and will play four simultaneous tables of $15–$30 on Party Poker. They can make upward of $200 an hour if the games are good. To make a similar rate playing live, they'd have to play $75–$150 limit, which is an enormous game by most standards. To reliably find games at these stakes, they'd have to live in Las Vegas or Atlantic City or Los Angeles. At the tables with those stakes they'd be forced to do battle with full-time world-class pros. I've never heard these guys speak of having aspirations to play that high.

And if they decide to play high-limit games online, there are plenty of options. Several sites offer tables that proffer buy-ins of $10,000 or more. One night on one particularly active table, I saw a player with $250,000 in his stack.

I enjoy online play, and if I choose to pursue a full-time poker career, there's no question that I'll put in a good number of hours online. With the exception of WPT stops and Vegas, where I could consistently find bad players who play high stakes, online is where I could make the most money with the least discomfort. I'd need to play in the evenings, when the sites are most active. But at least I'd get to spend time with Marisa between hands.

Playing online full-time would make for a solitary existence. I'd spend most of my days and nights in front of a computer, forever watching cards and clicking the mouse. In my years of contracting and writing I'd grown accustomed to long stretches alone and workdays without peers. I hadn't reported to an office for work in more than half a decade before I started the trip, and I had no desire to return any time soon.

I set off to Houston with continuing concerns about the state of my bankroll. Online play had gone well, and despite my indifference to the stakes, I had won more than $1,500 in the Dallas clubs. But I was still far short of my goal of $20,000 profit. My total take for the trip was just short of $8,000, leaving my bankroll right around $23,000. I was making progress, but I was running out of time. I had a month left on the trip, and a week of that would be spent in L.A. If I was going to get anywhere near my goal, I had to find big, juicy games every day. I could no longer waste time with short stacks or micro limits.

My first day in Houston only fueled my frustration. I found a club that ran a $100 buy-in tournament west of downtown. The tournament had among the worst structures I'd seen. The blinds started stupidly high and were raised every fifteen minutes. I busted early after a couple of bad beats, and moved to cash games. But once again the stacks were disappointingly low.

Houston was reputed to have a great poker scene, and I was determined to find a bigger game. I asked the club's managers, but they were reluctant to give me any information because they had no idea who I was. But I kept asking, indelicately prodding anyone who would listen for information. Finally a man who called himself Scooter said he could help me out. He knew of a $5-$10 pot-limit game that was half hold 'em, half Omaha that would run the following day. It was the first Monday afternoon game I'd heard of on my trip. It was a great game, he said. Very loose, very juicy.

Scooter popped out his cell phone and called a dealer who'd be working the game. I spoke to the dealer and made plans to meet him the following day. I'd drive to a specific intersection and call his cell. He'd then come get me and vouch for me within the club.

I arrived at the location at the appointed time, 12:45, and called. No answer. I left a message, waited fifteen minutes, and called again. Nothing. Dammit. From his description of the location, I determined the club was in the back of one of two strip malls. I drove around the parking lot of each until I found an unmarked door with multiple security cameras. This was it, no doubt, but I still didn't know how to proceed. Underground clubs are suspicious of strangers, those who just show up without anyone vouching for them. As it was Texas, I imagined some of these guys were armed.

After sitting for a few minutes and trying the dealer's cell yet again, I stopped a tall mustached man as he exited his massive pickup.

"Excuse me. Does Eric work here?"

"I don't know," he said, looking at me suspiciously.

I explained Eric was a dealer and I was supposed to meet him here. The man said he'd ask inside.

A minute later, a smiling pot-bellied man with a white turtle-neck and a baseball cap came to the parking lot. I explained that I had chatted with Eric.

"You looking to play?" he asked.

I nodded.

"Eric told me to expect you. Come on in," he said jovially.

I entered the plushest space I'd seen on the trip. The carpeting, decorated with a playing-card motif, was new. High-backed black leather chairs surrounded the two poker tables. And the wood-paneled walls were covered with well-framed prints of works of western art. Around the table men in their forties, fifties, and sixties sat quietly and sullenly. One man eyed me suspiciously.

"Somebody know him?" he asked the owner.

"He knows Scooter."

"Scooter? That motherfucker. He's been running so good lately. All of a sudden he thinks can play." He turned to me. "How d'ya know Scooter?"

"Tunica," I replied. I thought it best not to mention I'd only exchanged about twenty words with him the previous day.

"Mmm." He flashed an icy grimace then turned back to the table.

I sat silently on a comfortable black leather sofa waiting for a seat to open. After a short while the oldest man at the table—he must have been in his early seventies—got up, saying he was going for a long lunch. I was told I could play his seat while he was gone.

I bought $1,000 worth of chips and sat. Given the cool reception, I decided to offer little of my background. I wouldn't mention my experience as a player or the book. These guys didn't need to know I was a semipro or that I'd be documenting this game. If someone asked, I was in town for business.

The dealer, a kindly, bearded man, did ask, then followed up by wondering where I was from. New York, I told him, and in a flash he replied in a low murmur, "Get the rope."

I laughed heartily and he flashed a big smile. My ability to take a joke lightened the atmosphere. Before long there was a lively discussion with me and my city as the central topics. A man in his late fifties sitting directly to my left turned to me and talked extensively of his history with New York. His work had taken him to the Bronx with some frequency decades earlier.

"The problem with New York," he said, "is . . . there's nothing to do."

I didn't want to contradict him, but I was flummoxed. Nothing to do in New York?

I must have looked stymied because he immediately followed up, "There's no place to play golf . . . do outdoors stuff."

I quickly agreed. New York City is a lousy golf town.

When I asked what lines of work allowed this group to play poker on a Monday afternoon, I was given vague answers. "Business interests," one said. I didn't press the topic.

The cards treated me well. I saw pocket Aces in one of the first orbits and ended up pushing a short stack all-in preflop. He had Ace-King and I was up $400 in a matter of minutes. When I was offered delicious pot roast and tasty sides from an excellent local comfort-food joint, I got to thinking about how desirable the setup was. These guys had money to burn and nothing to do on a Monday afternoon but burn it. And they were happy for my good-natured company. For the first time on the trip, I was truly hustling—taking their money while providing some entertainment. This was fish hunting at its best.

When I was up $1,500 I decided to leave.

The same group would be there Thursday afternoon, and all seemed eager to have me back. "You come back here any time," the kindly dealer said. "You're the nicest New Yorker I've ever met," said one of the players. But I couldn't wait three days for the game, and I didn't have good leads for the other days of the week. Even after this win, I was still $10,500 short of my goal, of what I'd need to be competitive at the $10-$20 in Commerce. To make that kind of money I needed to find my way to a place where I could be sure to find quality games around the clock.

I was headed to Vegas.

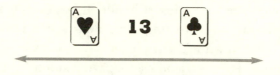

# 13

# LAS VEGAS

I WAS ELEVEN YEARS OLD ON MY FIRST TRIP TO LAS VEGAS. My mother, stepfather, stepsister, brother, and I were at the tail end of our see-the-West family trip that included stays at Bryce Canyon, Zion National Park, the Grand Canyon, Mesa Verde, and Pike's Peak. My memory of those natural wonders is limited—I have vague recollections of searing heat, steep climbs, and petrified wood. But my first encounter with Vegas lives vividly in my mind.

We stayed at the Maxim Hotel (closed in 1999), and as we walked through the lobby casino after check-in I was enthralled by the lights, the noise, the certainty of thrills the surroundings offered. We had two rooms, the kids in one, parents in the other. Once our luggage was parked, I was restless. I had no intention of staying put while there was so much excitement to be had just an elevator ride away.

I knocked on my mother's door and asked if I could go to the lobby. She said that I could but that I had to be back in ten minutes. My mother is not a gambling type—opera and poetry are her outlets. When I asked many years later if she regretted giving me this permission, she said, "It never occurred to me that it was not only a bad idea, but illegal for a minor to be in a casino."

So down I went, and just a hundred feet from the elevator door, there was a man putting silver dollars into two slot machines. I watched with fascination and asked why he was playing two machines. He was friendly enough and allowed me to watch as the machines paid off several times in succession. A security guard was not happy with my proximity to gaming equipment. "Sit down," he demanded, pointing to a bench that was within easy sight of the man and the slots. So I sat. For about a minute. Then I was up, ogling the money clanking into the silvery coin receptacle. The security guard, anger welling in his voice, insisted that I sit down; otherwise he'd have to have me removed. I sat.

Then the slot player had a request. "Kid, get me a cup." His winnings were substantial and he needed one of the casino-supplied plastic cups to hold his dollar coins. "I'll give you a buck."

I checked to see that the guard was otherwise engaged and bolted around a slot bank, looking for an unused cup. I quickly found one and returned it to the man. He held out a dollar and I said, "Play it." He shrugged, put it in the machine and pulled the lever.

"I'm not going to ask you again," the guard barked, as I was once again in front of the slots.

I sat. After a few beeps, the slot's spinning wheels came to a stop. "Hey, you won," the man said. My winnings—several dollars, I couldn't tell how many—fell from the body of the machine. The man pushed his own winnings into his cup and left. I now had a problem. Coins, my coins, my winnings, were in the coin basin of the slot machine. But the guard was looking directly at me.

I assessed the situation. The slot machine was only five or so feet from the bench on which I was sitting. I could get to the machine and fish out the coins in a matter of seconds. The elevator was a hundred feet beyond that. At a brisk walk I could cover the ground in ten seconds. The guard, taller and with a favorable angle, could beat me to the elevator. There was no question about that.

But would he want to? Would it be worth his time, his trouble to bust an eleven-year-old?

My read: No way.

I jumped to the slot, used both hands to grasp the numerous silver disks, and bolted to the elevator. I didn't look back, didn't give the man the opportunity for eye contact, a reason to scream, "Stop!"

I made it. The elevator reached our floor and when I reached my room, I spread the eleven silvery coins on the bed for my brother and stepsister to admire. I'd been in Vegas ten minutes and had an eleven-dollar profit. What a town. Why we were bothering with the Grand Canyon was completely beyond me.


After three days of hard driving through barren landscape and a brief stop at my aunt's in Albuquerque, I made it to Vegas. I checked in at the Sahara, a fashionable destination in the days of the Rat Pack that had suffered decades of neglect, and then drove directly to the Mirage. The Mirage has one of the more active poker rooms in Vegas, and as it was Saturday I didn't want to miss any weekend action. The poker room was lively. Most of the tables were filled, and floor managers were busy calling names and seating people. The list for the $2-$5 game was long, and for an hour I had nothing to do but loiter and people watch.

Just outside the poker room, a man walked by. He was forty or maybe forty-two, with a freshly trimmed black mustache and hair that was too neatly combed on top and just a couple inches short of a mullet in the back. The right side of his face was lined with a deep crevice. The sleeves of his shirt and sport jacket were cut to a precision length, and his fingers and wrists were well adorned with gold and diamonds. I'd seen the look before, at poker tables throughout the South. The statement of the fashion was clear enough: "I've done well," it said, "and I'd like you to be aware of it."

His companion was a cliché-inspiring beauty. Stunning, jaw-dropping, heartbreaking, traffic-stopping, ship-launching—they were all apt, but none did her justice. She was twenty-five, black, with light, taut, luminous skin. Subtly applied makeup accentuated her high cheeks and feline eyes. She wore a simple black cotton dress with pink piping that hinted at the fine figure beneath. Heads craned as she passed, as if Newtonian law demanded the reaction.

The pairing was bizarre—wrong. This man might very well have a fine-looking young woman on his arm, but she should wear conspicuous quantities of eye shadow and show prodigious cleavage. A dyed blonde seemed right. But there was no way this man belonged with a beauty of this simplicity and magnificence. I wondered what possible course of events could have led to the pairing.

Then I remembered. I was in Vegas. Beauty, like everything else, was for rent here.

In the poker room I sat at an empty table, perusing the latest copy of *Bluff* magazine while waiting for my name to be called. Three men in their late forties and early fifties gathered at the other end of the table. Two wore tracksuits; the other had on jeans that a tight belt kept affixed to his massive belly. They talked about the spread of the upcoming Super Bowl and how their picks had fared in the previous weeks of the NFL playoffs. Not well, from what I heard. The conversation then turned to poker, and they talked extensively about their earnings and beats over the previous days.

These guys, I could tell, were medium-stakes pros, grinders, who made their living at $20-$40 limit at the Mirage and maybe some $30-$60 at the Bellagio. I studied them from behind my magazine, knowing that if I were to play for a living in Vegas, my life would be like theirs. I'd know the floor men and the waitresses by name. My workday conversation with peers would cover odds on upcoming sporting events but would inevitably turn to a disaster card that cost me a pot. A lifetime of bad-beat stories—what a fate. I'd get fat. I'd already put on six pounds on this trip.

A game like $20-$40 would provide only a subsistence living, enough for me to pay bills and a mortgage and live comfortably in a city as cheap as Vegas. But with earnings of roughly $40 an hour, accumulating a bankroll for higher games would be very difficult—probably impossible. If I were younger, I could live cheaply and pour every possible dollar earned back into my roll, and I could take shots at bigger games and tournaments. But as an adult who wished to have a family, the wins at those limits would only support necessities.

The monotony would kill me. After a year, maybe two, there would be no intellectual challenge, no competitive thrill. My only goal would be to log hours and iterations with ill-equiped tourists. I'd make maybe five or six interesting decisions in a day. As I considered this course, I was certain I'd prefer to spend my days in a cubicle editing the text of some corporate magazine if it came to that. At least I'd have health insurance. Online play was a far preferable option.

My name was called for the $2-$5 no-limit game, and I took a seat next to one of the drunkest men I've ever played against. He had a full head of gray hair and an acne-scarred face. He asked me how I was, and I told him I was fine.

"You're a nice young man," he exclaimed instantly, his breath reeking of scotch and cigarettes. "Where are you from?"

"New York."

"I hate New York."

"Okay."

"I'm from up north."

"Canada?"

"Are you nuts? Reno. I'm from Reno."

"Okay. Good." I turned away, and he grasped my shoulder firmly.

"You're a nice young man. You just don't listen."

"Huh?"

"I don't mean to insult ya. . . . You're a good young man, but you don't listen at all."

"Okay."

"I like ya!" he said, and swatted my back in a manly, affectionate way. He quieted for a minute, then blurted with disgust, "You don't know nothing."

The maximum buy-in was $500, but there were several people at the table who had a good deal more on the table. I did a quick count; there was about $11,000 in play. Nice. There was real money to be won.

After only a dozen hands, I found 6♥-7♥ on the button. Two people had limped in front of me, and I raised to $25. Both limpers called.

The flop was about as good as I could hope for: Q♥-6♠-4♥.

I had a middle pair and a flush draw. My pair of 6s could very well be the best hand with that flop, and even if it wasn't best, my hand could easily improve. The early position limper, who had about $1,500 in front of him, checked, as did the other limper. I bet $60. The early position player then raised to $150. Damn. It was early in my session, so I didn't have a lot of information on how this guy played. In the time I'd been at the table he'd seen four flops—a very high percentage. When I looked at him, I saw that his curly black hair was matted and greasy and his eyes were slightly glassy. He might have been slightly drunk or maybe he hadn't slept in a day.

He could be bluffing, I thought, or he could have something like K-Q or Q-J. I really did not know. Finally I decided I didn't much care what he had and moved all-in. If he had just one pair he might fold, and if not, I still had plenty of outs. A classic semi-bluff. Even if I lost, burning a buy-in so early could do wonders for my table image. He called instantly. Woops.

"Set?" I asked. I was sure I was dead.

"No, I'm sure I'm crushed," was his reply. Really? Then why call? He turned over A♥-5♥.

When I saw his cards—the better flush draw, the Ace—I was certain I'd lose this pot. For some reason, I assumed that I'd already lost, that I was drawing dead. I reached into my pocket and pulled out my roll. As I was peeling off bills, I noticed a pile of chips heading my way. The dealer was pushing me the pot. What? I looked at the board: Q♥-6♠-4♥-K♦-2♠. My pair of 6s was best. Nice.

A short while later I called a $40 bet on the flop with nothing more than a gut-shot straight draw. I hit and took $450 from my opponent, who held pocket Aces. In my peripheral vision I noticed shaking heads. My tablemates had drawn the only possible conclusion: I was both lucky and reckless.

The player to my immediate left, a tall, angular man with a stack with more than $2,500, seemed particularly eager to take me down a peg. Several times I limped and he pounced with oversized raises. A couple of times I called his raises, hoping to hit a flop, but I missed and had to surrender when faced with huge flop bets.

Then I saw my first big hand of the night, K♣-K♠, while on the button. It was folded to me, and I raised to $20. The player to my left mumbled something about my frequent raises—in just a few hours this guy had learned to despise me. He called from the small blind. The big blind also called.

The flop: J♣-7♦-4♦.

The small blind bet out $60. Big blind folded, and I raised to $250. I wanted the message to be clear here: I have a hand—no bluff this time. The response: five black chips. It would cost me another $250 to call. I stopped; it was time to think. This is the type of spot where a bad player will unthinkingly throw his chips in the pot. He'll look at his Kings and say, "I have a great hand" without considering his opponent's cards.

And I had plenty to consider. There was no question in my mind that he had a hand. The raise was too small for a semi-bluff with a diamond draw and was way too small for an effective outright bluff. Could the small raise be an invitation to call? Did he hit a set and was he looking for me to commit my $1,220? Or was the bet weak? Was the $250 small enough so that he could get out if I reraised? Either scenario seemed plausible.

His raise came extremely quickly. The chips landed in front of him only seconds after my bet. If he had a monster hand, he'd likely take some time to figure how he could best extract the most from my remaining stack. That argued against a set. I then reviewed the betting in my mind and stopped on what I thought was the key action: his initial $60 bet. Would this guy bet out with a set of 7s? An expert would make that play, knowing that if he gets raised he's likely to win a very large pot. But a novice—and I thought this guy was at best a novice—looks at his huge hand and becomes concerned with frightening his opponents off; he slow-plays or check-raises with the hope of getting some value—any value—out of the big hand. The more I thought about that initial bet, the more I thought a set was unlikely. Then there was my table image; he thought I was capable of bluffing at any time. I decided only one holding was feasible: Ace-Jack, he had top-pair, top kicker, and thought I was trying to bluff him.

"I'm all-in," I said. A look of shock came across his face. He asked for a count and when he saw it was $720 more, he froze. His delay made it clear I had made the right choice. Eventually, he folded.

I ended my first day in Vegas with a tidy $1,400 profit.

I returned to the Mirage the next day, eager to play in their Sunday tournament—with its $330 buy-in with $200 rebuys. A year and a half earlier, I won the Sunday tournament when it was slightly cheaper and added $4,500 to my bankroll, by far my largest win at the time.

I love the early stages of tournaments. When blinds are low compared with the size of the stacks, my cash-game expertise gives me a significant edge over most competition. When I have a stack with $1,500 in tournament chips, and the blinds are $5-$10, I can call a raise—which will typically be in thirty to fifty chip range—with the hope of either hitting a flop or outplaying the competition as the hand progresses. In the early rounds of the Mirage tournament I was able to pad my stack nicely without risking much or even hitting cards. In one typical hand, a man raised in middle position. I called in the big blind with 8-9. The flop of 7-4-2 didn't have an Ace, King, or Queen, so I figured if the raiser didn't have a high pocket pair, he'd fold if I bet. That's exactly what happened. My initial table was perfect for these sorts of plays. Most were too tight and a little scared.

But as tournaments continue, the blinds rise. Playing any hand requires a greater portion of one's stack. When, say, 20 percent of a player's chips are heading into the pot with the preflop action, there tends to be very little postflop play. This is quite reasonable. With so little money remaining in the stacks, it's impossible to get paid in proportion to the risk when starting as an underdog. For example, in a cash game, I'd happily call a raise and see a flop with pocket 5s, even if I knew my opponent had pocket Aces. I might be a 7-to-1 underdog to hit that set on the flop, but if I do hit, I might get paid off at a 20-to-1 rate. In the middle and later stages of a tournament, there's simply no way to make the math work; the stacks aren't deep enough to get paid in proportion to the risk. In general, later in tournaments nobody wants to go into the flop with the second-best hand. So starting with the best cards—or giving the appearance of starting with the best cards—is critical. Thus aggression becomes vital. The preflop

attacker—the first one to raise—will often steal the blinds without a fight. A player who fails to steal blinds will see his stack
whittled away to nothing.

At the midstages of the Mirage tournament, I took decent-
sized pots with pocket Js and pocket 9s—hands that can often lead
to a lot of trouble. When my stack was in decent shape, I got aggressive, raising at least one hand per orbit, sometimes two or
three. On a couple of occasions I reraised from the blinds, making
it clear that stealing from me would not be easy. After two and a
half hours of play, I had $10,000 in tournament chips. I wasn't the
chip leader, but I was in good shape.

With the blinds at $200-$500, I was feeling very comfortable.
Most of the players at my table had been there for some time,
and I had a solid sense of how they played. With a few well-
timed steals, I thought I'd be able to make it to the final table.
Then I saw A♠-Q♥ in early position, and raised $1,250. I was
called by the only woman at the table, who was in the small
blind. She had a soccer mom sort of look, and was very friendly.
She often showed her cards after winning a pot, even when there
was no showdown. Each time she showed a very good hand. So
her call from the small blind was a shock. I needed to proceed
with caution.

The flop was Q♣-7♣-4♣.

I had top pair, top kicker, but I had no club—no flush draw.
Before I could think about how I wanted to proceed, she
moved in, pushed her remaining $4,700 in front of her. I im-
mediately apologized to the table, telling them that my decision
would take a while, that I had a lot to think about. Did I have
the best hand? Probably. She wouldn't have made such a huge
bet if she had flopped the Ace-high flush. But she almost certainly had the Ace of clubs, the card that would guarantee her a
victory if a fourth club hit on the turn or river. If she had either
an off-suit King or a seven along with her A♣, she'd have
enough outs to give her an almost 50 percent chance of winning

the hand. The question I confronted was relatively simple: *At this point in the tournament, did I want to flip a coin for half my stack?*

Eighteen players were left in the tournament; the top nine would cash. My stack was in decent shape and I was effectively stealing. In fact, I felt I had good control over my table. This was not the time to gamble, I decided. I threw my cards away.

"Ace of clubs with a queen?" I asked.

"I had the ace," she said. The other card would remain a mystery.

Fifteen minutes later the blinds rose to $500 and $1,000, and I'd failed to increase my stack. I had only $8,500 after posting the big blind, and thirteen players remained. It was folded to a player in late position who moved in his remaining $4,500 chips. In the big blind I saw a pair of 8s. I knew exactly where I stood. He had two overcards, maybe something like A-9 or K-Q, and he wanted me to fold; he wanted to steal. My pocket pair was an ever-so-slight favorite against such a hand, but essentially it was a coin flip. Once again, I had to decide if I wanted to gamble.

At this point my calculation was slightly different. Some of the stacks had gotten very large. If I won this hand, the additional chips would help me compete with the big stacks, but if I lost, I'd be in desperate shape and risked finishing out of the money. I decided to call; the opponent showed Q-T, and I was lucky enough that he didn't hit a pair. My hand held up. Soon, we were down to the final nine. I was in the money.

The Mirage used a typical payout schedule for their tournaments in which the top three places made far more than everyone else. For this tournament ninth through fifth places all paid between $1,200 and $3,000. Then the prizes rose steadily. Third paid $4,700; second $7,800; and first $10,300.

As play got underway I was reminded how horribly inelegant final tables are in small tournaments. They have no resemblance to what viewers see on World Poker Tour and World

Series of Poker telecasts. Generally, the blinds are so high that most, if not everyone, at the table is sacrificing a huge portion of their stack with each round of blinds. The sight of an Ace in the hole—no matter the kicker—is usually enough to prompt a short or moderate stack to move all-in and pray that no one will call. Swings in stacks sizes are monumental as short stacks bust or double up.

At this stage luck is a far greater factor than skill. And I was getting lucky. I saw some decent cards that allowed me to double up early in the final table play. I was equally fortunate to have Ron, the chip leader, to my right. Ron, who had almost half the chips in play, was a horrible poker player. He never raised, but he was willing to call almost any bet with any cards. This is a horrid strategy, but Ron was getting lucky, eliminating player after player.

With the blinds at $1,000 and $2,000 I had a stack of about $15,000. Ron limped—a sin in late-stage tournament poker that he repeated constantly—and I found pocket Kings. I moved in and everyone else folded to Ron, who called. He showed K-J, and I doubled up.

A short while later, with the blinds at $2,000-$5,000, it was folded around to Ron in the small blind, who once again limped. I saw K♥-T♥ and moved in for another $20,000. He called and turned over his Q-7. The table was shocked to see his cards. Why would he call with that hand? It made no sense. I paired the ten on the turn, and suddenly I was the chip leader.

With the blinds swallowing the three shorter stacks alive, I had no choice but to surrender my blinds when I saw a couple of rounds of wretched cards. Ron continued to call everything— and he hit, eliminating the three other players. By the time we got heads-up, when we were playing for first place—I was at an almost four-to-one chip disadvantage: my $30,000 to his $120,000.

I raised aggressively every time I had the opportunity, but I was just treading water, managing to maintain but not build my stack. With $7,000 in blinds posted every two hands, I was in constant jeopardy. I knew I could outplay Ron, but there was almost no room for strategy given my stack and the blinds. After about fifteen hands, Ron raised on the button, and I saw Q-T. This was not a great hand—I was likely a statistical underdog. I decided that the hand was strong enough to gamble with. I simply couldn't surrender my big blind with a hand of that strength. And if I got lucky and won this hand, I thought I'd have a decent shot to win. I moved all-in, and of course, Ron called. He showed A-4. The dealer put out the flop: 4♦-J♣-K♥.

No help. The turn: 7♥. And the river: 6♠.

Ron won. But I felt no jealousy when the tournament manager handed me $7,800 in cash. After the tip and buy-in, I'd made $7,200 in profit.

A year and a half earlier, when I won $4,500 in the Mirage tournament, I was at a loss over what to do with the pile of money that was handed to me. It was so unwieldy and bulky, I asked for an envelope. I'd learned some things in that year and a half. This time, I nonchalantly asked for a rubber band. I folded the stack of bills in half, doubled the rubber band over it and slipped the mass into my left front pocket.

Exhausted and hungry, I went to the Mirage café to get a bite and a beer and to relax. As I ate my Greek salad, Ron wandered in, and I asked him to join me. He was a sweet, soft-spoken guy who owned a graphics shop in Minneapolis. It was, he said, his very first tournament. I believed him. If he continued to act as a calling station in future tournaments he'd have horrible results. But I was there to celebrate with him, not to critique his play.

As we chatted, he said one of the sweetest things any straight man has said to me. "You know, I was really confident that entire tournament, but when I had to face you heads-up—I got really scared."

I smiled. Pride welled within me.

---

I returned to the Sahara and laid out the money that I had in my travel bankroll. I made piles of $1,000. Most had ten $100 bills, but others had a few hundred in $20s. I placed the piles end-to-end at right angles, like dominoes. There on the bed was $14,460. I'd been in Vegas only thirty-six hours and I had won $8,600.

My winnings for the trip were now just shy of $18,000.

# 14

# LAS VEGAS, PART II

I BELIEVE IT'S UNFAIR THAT I HAVE TO PAY TAXES AT THE same rate as the rest of the American population. This isn't some nutty libertarian antitax view. My leanings are more socialist than libertarian, actually, and I believe Americans are greatly undertaxed, given what we ask of the government. Moreover, I believe I have societal and ethical responsibilities to pay my fair share. My complaint is that, as a poker player, money means entirely different things to me than it does to the rest of the American populace— or the IRS.

For nongamblers, income relates proportionally to spending power. If a person with a regular job saw a two–day $8,600 windfall, as I did in Vegas, his thoughts would immediately focus on how the money could be most effectively disbursed—to vacations, debt reduction, toys, or even mutual fund purchases. But I couldn't think about using my winnings for something as practical as a down payment for a condo or as whimsical as a lengthy East-Asian jaunt. The money had more immediate uses.

Primarily it would serve as a barrier against bankruptcy. As the beginning of this trip proved, I'm capable of losing for prolonged periods. The deeper my bankroll, the less panicky I'd feel when nasty streaks came my way: losing $5,000 from a $40,000 bankroll would be less traumatic than seeing the same amount disappear from a bankroll half that size. The money would also provide the opportunity for playing higher. If I wanted to play that $10-$20 game in Los Angeles, I'd need to reinvest nearly every cent of the money I'd won.

To claim my winnings at the Mirage tournament, I had to hand over my driver's license and fill out a 1099 form. At the end of the year, if I didn't have documented losses to show the IRS, I'd pay taxes on that tournament as I would if the sum had come from a contracting gig. I couldn't tell the IRS that I'd put every dollar in my bankroll, that I needed that money to keep me safe, that the money would increase my earning power. In a way it wasn't income at all, because I couldn't spend it. But I wouldn't want to try to explain these theories to an IRS auditor. And, for that matter, I think my left-leaning friends would listen to this argument and respond with phrases like, "Pay your taxes, you fucking hypocrite."

Beyond taxes, I don't think most could easily comprehend the multiple and paradoxical views of money I'd developed in the course of my poker life. As my game progressed, I grew increasingly cavalier about inflows and outflows of cash at the table. I bluffed more frequently and made more speculative calls. This ensured bigger swings, as those types of plays involved more risk. But as experience made me a better player, I was capable of making tougher, gutsier decisions because I was better able to determine the likely profitability of any action. Of course I made some costly mistakes, but on the whole I was making far more good decisions than bad ones. And when I was playing well, I focused solely on the criteria that would help me determine the proper play, without giving any thought to the off-table value of the money. I carried a residual understanding that my chips were precious: I desired to protect those that I had and accumulate those I didn't. Without this memory, there would have been no sense of consequences. I'd throw money in every pot without regard to the outcome. But if I stopped to consider the real-world value of my chips—the rent or bills or engagement rings I could buy—I would have been far less willing to make the tough but necessary crying call or raise on nothing but a sense of an opponent's weakness. The better I became, the more easily the money flowed.

Yet in my everyday life I became far more concerned with the cost of things. To put it simply, I became a cheapskate. I didn't travel other than to poker tournaments or purchase big-ticket items. I didn't even buy new clothes. Marisa and I ate out more frequently than we should have, but that was the extent of my wastefulness. At times I had piles of cash around the apartment that I refused to spend.

The dual treatments of money, while strange, provided evidence of a certain maturity and mental health, I think. If I allowed my at-the-table attitude toward money to seep into the rest of my life, I'd be a mess. Like so many top-flight pros who wander around tournament rooms broke, I'd piss away all of my winnings, justifying my profligacy by offering poker comparisons: "Hey, I bluffed off ten times that last night!" "You think that's expensive? You should have seen what that flush on the river cost me last night." The excuses to spend would be endless, and I would constantly be broke. The fact that I could be shocked by the $1,700 theft before the start of the trip and by the $27 Platinum Package at Graceland was good news. I maintained my appreciation for the value of money.

When, the day after my tournament win, I wandered through the Grand Canal Shoppes at the Venetian, stopping in jewelry stores that offered engagement rings, my sense of money was fully intact. The selections started at $9,000. I nodded politely at a saleswoman when she told me this. She shrugged, and I turned to leave.


When most poker players travel to Vegas, they head to one of two casinos, the Mirage or the Bellagio. These are the storied poker spots, the ones where you're supposed to find the best and biggest action. But with poker's burgeoning popularity, many of the other casinos opened rooms. Mandalay Bay, Luxor, Excalibur, Sahara, Flamingo, Aladdin, MGM Grand—by 2005 they all advertised their poker rooms as a way to lure the new wave of players. The Wynn, the ridiculously opulent resort that opened in 2005 a few months after my trip, made great efforts to promote their room and has even tried to lure the biggest games away from the Bellagio. In one of the more interesting publicity initiatives in poker history, Wynn hired Dan Negreanu to be their poker ambassador. He agreed to play cash games only at the Wynn. Rumors around the poker world put his salary at somewhere between $600,000 and $3 million, but nobody knows for sure. As soon as the Wynn opened, Negreanu put out an open challenge: He'd play any player in the world heads-up at the game of his or her choosing for stakes starting at $2,000-$4,000 limit. As of the writing of this book, Negreanu was not doing especially well in the challenges, having lost a majority of the initial seven matches. This outcome was predicted by many, for no matter how good Negreau may be (and he is without question one of the best players in the world), when he allows other great players to chose their preferred games, he starts with a profound disadvantage. It's hard to see how any player could profitably manage such situations over a long period.

There was no reason for me to play anything at Excalibur or Sahara—the stakes just weren't high enough. But ignoring everything outside of the Mirage or the Bellagio could have been a huge mistake. Besides, the action at the big rooms wasn't guaranteed to be great. The Bellagio, in particular, was problematic for me. They spread a variety of limit games—everything from $2-$4 to $400-$800—but had only two levels of no-limit. Their $2-$5 no-limit game required a $200 buy-in, no more, no less. I had enough evidence at this point in the trip to conclude that I was, in fact, a losing player when the stakes dropped too low.

The only other no-limit game had $10 and $20 blinds and was held in the slightly elevated and guarded high-limit area. The first night I was at the Bellagio, I saw that if I bought into that game, I could sit at a table adjacent to the one where Jen Harmon and Phil Ivey were playing. They were probably involved in the biggest game on the planet—the $4,000-$8,000 rotation game that drew only the most talented players and the wealthiest fish. A bad night at that game could result in a $1 million loss.

There are only about a dozen people in the world who regularly play that high, and according to Barry Greenstein, only he and four other people beat the game on a regular basis: Phil Ivey, Chip Reese, Chau Giang, and Doyle Brunson. I have no illusions that I'll ever be one of the five best players in the world, that I'll ever be competitive with the likes of Ivey or Greenstein. But the $10-$20 no-limit was almost within reach. My bankroll was nearly there. Before too long, barring any serious reversals, I'd be able to play the high-limit room at Bellagio. I'd be able to sit just a few feet from the game's elite.

But not that night. I still had a few weeks left on my trip and I didn't want to put eight or nine thousand in play, which is what I'd need to do if I were to play the $10-$20 Bellagio game. The higher stakes would wait for Commerce.

For lively medium-stakes action, I headed slightly off the Strip, to one of the newest casinos in Vegas—the Palms. The Palms has been promoting itself as an ultra-hip, young, sexy spot. Their waitresses, in eye-catching fetishistic leather ensembles, are the hottest in town and their nightclubs are reputed to be among the best. The Palms was also the host of *Celebrity Poker Showdown*. When I arrived and headed to the poker room, I passed by a roped-off area where a television taping was in progress. The Speed Channel had gathered great NASCAR drivers to compete in a poker tournament. I was slightly awed by the concept and wondered what the next step in televised poker might be. I imagined a PBS pledge-week special that featured the Three Tenors, Yanni, and Michael Flatley battling at the felt.

The Palms had two small poker rooms—one with four tables, the other with seven. In the larger of the two, they spread low-limit games—$2-$4, $3-$6 limit. The other room they dubbed the "high-limit" area, and on most nights it was dedicated exclusively to $2-$5 no-limit. That game drew a strange combination of ready-to-party Angelenos and locals. The Vegas-area players that I met at the Palms were of a slightly different breed than most I'd encountered in other casinos. In the poker rooms at the Mirage and the Bellagio, I ran into the grinders—the $15-$30 and $20-$40 pros. And at places like Palace Station, where the limits never got higher than $4-$8 limit, there was a homier feel—a place where low-level casino workers got together to pass some time after finishing their shifts. But at the Palms, the locals were a lot like the guys I'd seen in underground clubs around the country. They had jobs—real estate, local television, law—and they came to this room for action.

On the first night I played at the Palms there was no shortage of huge pots. It seemed no raise was big enough to thin the field. Each pot was contested by three, four, or five players, with as much as $300 going into the pot before the flop. Early on, I had my pocket Kings cracked by Ace-Jack. But that was fine. I knew this was a game where I expected big swings. I started down $500, built up a $200 profit, but ended the evening with a $300 loss.

In one perplexing encounter that night, a hefty young black man dressed in white pants, white shirt, white floppy hat, and a fair amount of bling got into a screaming match with a scraggly, grizzled local. I had no idea how the argument started, but by the time it reached a volume audible to all, available wealth was the core issue.

"What I got on is worth more than your bankroll!" the young man screamed, pointing to the diamond-studded pendant attached to the thick gold chain around his neck.

"Yeah, I believe that. And who fucking cares?" responded the local.

"I got a hundred-thousand-dollar Hummer outside, mother-fucker."

"Like I fuckin' care."

The argument continued like this for a good five minutes. Each party assured the other that he would, in due time, fuck the other party up. The floor man watched the spectacle and chatted with a waitress as the argument escalated. I thought they might come to blows, but neither of these combatants seemed ready for a physical altercation. The local probably realized he was well out of his weight class. The Hummer owner, I guessed, would not want to dirty any part of his perfectly white outfit.

My second night at the Palms started strangely. Despite the $500 maximum buy-in, a number of players had well over $1,000 in front of them. Clearly, there'd been a fair amount of rebuying. One of the owners of a big stack was a young man, maybe twenty-three, who looked a little like the actor Seth Green. He sat immediately to my left and was drinking hard. His girlfriend, a very pretty young Chinese woman with a hip denim outfit and long hair with blond highlights, was seated behind him. She seemed ready for a night of clubbing, and squirmed restlessly in her chair.

In the first orbit I played, Seth opened with a raise to $25 in about half the hands, and in most of those he was called in two or three spots. This was a wide-open table, and if I managed to hit some cards, I could make a killing. I saw trash the first orbit and folded.

In the small blind I found pocket 2s. True to form, Seth, who was under the gun, raised to $25. There were two middle-position callers, and then the man on the button reraised to $45. This was a bizarre, almost pointless raise. By raising only $20 he pretty much ensured that everyone who was in for $25 would throw in an extra $20. The pot would be too big, too tempting for a fold.

Normally, after a raise and a reraise, pockets 2s should be thrown in the muck without hesitation. But I wasn't eager to fold. Seth probably had nothing and would just call the additional $20, and the other players in the hand would likely do the same. So $40 was likely all I'd have to contribute preflop. And with the amount of money that was in preflop, there was a good chance that by the river this pot would be huge. I decided to gamble and tossed out the $40 call.

The flop was: 3♠-4♥-5♦.

Not the best flop for me, but not the worst either. I had a draw, with an Ace or a 6 giving me a straight. But this was a dangerous draw at best, as a 6 would make me a straight but would give anyone with a 7 a better straight. I checked and Seth bet out $75. A player in middle position called, as did the button. Then it was back to me. I thought about the $75 bet. What could that possibly mean? It was only about one quarter of the pot, not nearly enough to get anyone with a straight draw or an overpair to fold. Even if he had an overpair, maybe 9s, he'd want to protect it with a bet that was at least half the pot, probably more. The only hand where he'd want to invite calls was with 6-7, the nuts. But I couldn't believe he had that. This guy would check the nuts, slow-play, I thought.

What was I to make of the calls? Anyone with any sort of draw would call—any 6 or 7. Mostly I thought these guys were sticking around without much of anything. They were just hoping the turn would bring a card that would give them a chance at this large pot.

Even having decided that nobody had a particularly big hand, there was still a question for me: What was I prepared to do about the weakness I sensed? I almost certainly did not have the best hand—there had to be a pair better than 2s out there somewhere—and it was reasonably likely that someone had a good draw. I determined that my stack was deep enough to force folds by those who held the straight draw or any single pair. If my raise looked convincing enough they might assume that I flopped the straight. So I raised. "Three hundred," I announced.

Seth folded quickly, and one middle-position player called off his last $100 in chips. I had simply failed to notice the size of that player's stack. If I had seen it, I wouldn't have made the play. If that guy had any hand—any pair, any draw—he'd certainly call another $100. The pot was far too big for him to fold for that sum. The button folded. I figured I was behind, but still had some outs—maybe the Ace or a 6.

The turn was the 4♦, and the river was the J♠, leaving a board of 3♠-4♥-5♦-4♦-J♠. When the dealer asked for our cards I sheepishly showed my 2s, and the lone remaining player said, "They're good," and tossed his hand in the muck.

The table was shocked. I was thrilled. I'd won a nice pot and developed a great table image. I was able to get paid nicely when I hit a couple of hands that night and added another $1,000 to my bankroll.

On Wednesday I played in the Bellagio $500 buy-in tournament, where I played my sharpest poker of the trip. I saw opportunities more clearly than I had at any point in the previous months. In one encounter, when the blinds were $150-$300, I was in the small blind and everyone folded to me. I held J♠-T♦ and matched the big blind, who then checked. The flop was A♠-A♣-6♥. I checked and the big blind quickly bet $500. I was certain he held nothing—no Ace, no pair. The bet was a little too big and a little too forceful. And as soon as I saw his bet, I knew exactly how the hand would play out. I'd call his $500, and that action would scare him to death. It would look as if I were slow-playing trip Aces. Then I'd check the turn and he'd check behind me, certain I was looking to check-raise him. Then on the river I'd bet half the pot, make it look as though I was trying to squeeze a little extra value out of the hand, and he'd fold.

That's exactly what happened.

I made it to the final two tables of that tournament, but failed to cash in when I played a massive three-way pot with a monster draw that didn't connect. When my chips went into that pot with two overcards, a gutshot, and a flush draw, I was certain that if I hit, I'd make it to the final table. In fact, I liked my chances of winning this one, but I missed. Still, I was playing well and feeling great.

In the final months of our dying marriage, my ex-wife and I traded any number of unfair and bitter accusations. Every flaw we saw was exaggerated in each other's eyes, and when things were at their worst, we had no compunctions about overstating a defect and framing it in the most hurtful way we could devise. After a few years and happier times, I've been able to compartmentalize much of what I was accused of in those days and sort those that had legitimacy from those that did not. I hope and believe that my ex, now remarried and a mother, has been able to do the same.

Without question the most enduring of her criticisms, the one that always seemed legitimate, even in our deepest rages, concerned my unevenness of mood. To listen to her, my happiness on any given day was largely determined by external factors. If I had a good day at work, I was a charming and energetic companion. If I had a bad day—had some sort of nasty confrontation with a coworker—I was a pill, difficult, a lousy person to be around. The inconsistency, she said, was deeply unfair to her.

I never disagreed with this, and made this trait the focus of much of the therapy that followed my marriage. I feel that learning the simple phrase *Control what you can* has been worth the thousands that my insurance wouldn't cover.

Though I finished my therapy long before I started seriously with poker, I wonder what Dr. Hermann might divine from this choice. *Why,* he might ask, *would a person who claims to have difficulty managing his moods choose a line of work that is certain to inflict mood-altering episodes at an alarming rate? If you're actually interested in being a more consistent and stable companion, Jay, why not put yourself in less volatile situations? And really, what could possibly be more volatile than what you chose?*

Like any competent shrink Dr. Hermann would let me come to the obvious answer myself: I like living like this. I enjoy the exaggerated moods. The stabs of emotion that accompany the fall of the cards—the ones that win me a tournament or cost me a huge pile of cash—fill me with an energy I find nourishing. This is how I want my life to be. Even if I were to stop playing cards, I'd find my way to some avocation that offered seismically shifting foundations.

When I called Marisa from Vegas the night of my tournament win, she shared my joy in the same way she shared my despair when I was in Atlantic City. As always, she was capable of finding the perfect counterpoise to my moment's mood, but this is not a service I can ask her to perform for the remainder of her life. As I learned the first time through, there are limits to what one should expect from a spouse. Marisa will get sick of it eventually, as well she should.

So in going forward, whether with poker or without, I must find a way to compartmentalize my need for severe emotional shifts with my obligations to my mate. Perhaps the realization of these needs is all I'll need to start addressing the conflicts. Maybe knowing that at some level I desire the bad beat will help me remember that I don't need to share its aftermath. It's a joy that's mine alone.

My final day in Vegas I returned to the Mirage in the middle of the afternoon. There was a $2–$5 game going, but what really piqued my interest was the list for a $5–$10 game that would likely start within an hour. To kill time, I sat in the $2–$5 game and started the session bluffing. I raised with Q–T in late position and was called. I missed the 7-high flop completely, but bet anyway. I was check-raised, but the raise was small, and I decided that my opponent was weak and reraised. He thought, then went all-in. I folded and he showed me his pocket 3s as he raked the pot.

*Slow down, Jay,* I warned myself. *You must look way too eager if you're getting caught in that spot.*

When the $5-$10 game was announced, I moved immediately and bought the maximum—$1,000, as did most everyone else. It was a cordial but quiet crew, and without question the toughest table I'd seen in Las Vegas. I didn't play many hands for the first two hours—a combination of solid, aggressive opponents and mediocre cards kept me quiet. The most detailed conversation I had was with the young man to my left who ordered a black tea with seven sugars, and, upon completion of that, ordered another.

"I think you've had enough," I said.

"What?"

"Look, I don't know you, but I'm concerned."

"Yeah?"

"Diabetes, tooth decay. You know what I'm saying."

He nodded and we got back to cards.

While sitting in early position I was dealt pocket Queens, my best hand in hours. Before it was my turn to act, the under-the-gun player raised to $30. Of course, Queens is a solid pre-flop hand, but the raiser in this hand was obscenely tight. I didn't think he'd raise with much of anything under-the-gun. So I decided to proceed cautiously and called. Then the player on the button, a New Yorker of roughly my age who'd shown himself to have considerable skill, raised to $100. In this situation, I had no doubt that the reraiser had a very good hand. The under-the-gun player folded and it was back to me. I didn't quite have it in me to fold pocket Queens, so I called.

The flop was A♣-7♦-6♥.

With an ace staring me in the face, it was pretty clear that I was behind: He had either Kings or Ace-King, most likely. So I checked, and the other player checked behind me. The turn was the T♠. I checked once again, and my opponent bet $225. That bet stopped me in my tracks. Why bet so strong after checking the flop? Maybe he hated that Ace as much as I did and was now trying to put an end to the hand after I showed weakness by checking on both the flop and the turn. He must have pocket Kings, I reasoned, and I can make him fold. "I'm all-in," I announced and pushed my remaining $780 into the pot.

"Call," he said immediately, and without prompting he flipped over his pocket Aces. He had a set of bullets, and I was drawing dead.

The other players were slack-jawed when they saw my hand. When I cashed out, one player suggested that I come back. "It was fun playing with you," he said. I knew the act: Treat the fish nicely so that maybe they'll come back. I was the hunted.

The $1,300 I lost on the day served as a forceful reminder that I needed to show some humility and leave some room for error at the table. But I wasn't about to be especially critical of myself. The week in Vegas had treated me brilliantly. I was headed to the Golden State with total winnings of $16,700, only $2,300 short of my goal.

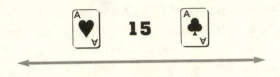

# SAN FRANCISCO

I HEADED OUT OF VEGAS AND THROUGH THE VAST NEVADA and California desert with more than $15,000 in hundred-dollar bills beneath my driver's seat. I was headed to San Francisco, my former home, where I'd see some old friends and play in the clubs where my poker life started. After six hours of austere landscapes I stopped at a Best Western along Interstate 5. Upon checking in I asked for a safe-deposit box, and the counter attendant, a wonderfully friendly woman in her midforties, said that would be no problem. She gathered a couple of keys and then her head disappeared beneath the counter. The sounds of struggle started immediately—grunting and bashing, followed momentarily by a resigned "Damn!"

"Maybe you'll have better luck with this. I can't get it open," she said as she stood.

I walked behind the counter and saw the safe-deposit box enclosure. It was small—maybe a foot high and eighteen inches deep—and contained three small doors that required two keys each. When I tried to work the keys in each of the locks, twisting with some force, the enclosure moved from side to side. It couldn't have weighed more than twenty pounds and was unattached to the counter—no bolts, no screws. "Never mind," I said.

"You sure? We can probably get it to work."

"No, it's all right," I said, and refrained from noting that a safe-deposit box that could be carried away under one arm did not offer the protections I sought. In my room, I tucked the wads of bills beneath my mattress.

The following day I was up before 6:00 and was eager to get on the road. With only a few hours of driving time remaining, I had the opportunity to indulge in one of my favorite San Francisco activities—drinking a dark, rich cup of coffee while reading the paper at one of the myriad quality coffee shops I knew. Before 9:00, I was sitting along Church Street drinking myself jittery while reading the national edition of *The New York Times.* I couldn't have been happier.

Later that day I went to the Presidio, where my friends Kathy and Mike were throwing a birthday party for their four-year-old, Simone, at a bowling alley. The scene was wonderfully chaotic. A dozen children eagerly pushed balls toward the pins. The felling of more than two was cause for great celebration. One group of parents maintained safety on the lanes while other parents snapped pictures.

I looked on with adult friends I hadn't seen in a couple of years. We caught up—a couple of job changes, one pregnancy, one broken relationship. The conversation was adult and intimate, and I enjoyed it immensely. And there were a few friends of Kathy's that I hadn't met, including a couple, Robert and Denise, with whom I shared some small talk. I learned quickly that Robert was a carpenter who ate only organic food and never watched TV. I think he mentioned his lack of interest in TV three times in ten minutes.

When he asked about my line of work, I told him about poker and the book. I'd come to enjoy such conversations. Most people are fascinated by the concept of poker as a profession and will ask questions with an amused curiosity. I answer straight-faced, as I would if I were describing my life as a middle manager. I feel a satisfaction in the smiles I encounter, knowing that my job is, by most standards, pretty cool.

But Robert responded with a sneer. "You play poker? How much money do you play for?"

I told him the stakes.

"You must have some . . . *inclination* for that kind of thing," he said. I could hear disapproval in his voice.

"I guess I do."

He nodded.

I couldn't pinpoint the source of Robert's disgust. He might have been showing an ultraliberal's reflexive disdain for all things less meaningful than the few activities he deems worthy—reading, mountain biking, composting, pot smoking. I moved on, feeling no desire to be judged by a sanctimonious pseudohippy.

I did mention the name of the book, but I had to wonder if any of Robert's feelings had to do with the concept behind fish hunting. More than once I had asked myself, Is this a way for a decent person to make a living? Or to phrase the question more harshly: Can someone who continually exploits the comparative ignorance and stupidity of those around him be considered a good person? I've raised some version of this question with my peers, other pros and semipros. They dismissed me as foolish. The fish, they say, know what they're getting themselves into. They're aware that they may be at a skill disadvantage, but they come because they want to compete, and we're doing nothing wrong by offering the competition.

This reasoning is unconvincing. Compared to some fish I'd played against on this trip, the differences in skill were so great that there was no way our interactions could be viewed as competitive. The fish were bound to lose; I'd win, there was no alternative outcome. It was a blowout, a rout. In any other test of skill—bowling, chess, tennis, Trivial Pursuit—a similar disparity in ability would be obvious to all participants in minutes. In boxing, there'd be a death. But in poker, with its prolonged sessions and swings and short-term luck, a lesser player can convince himself that he can come out ahead. Of course I know better, yet I let the fish stay ignorant. So even if I assume that the people I'm playing against are fully cognizant of their risks, what am I to make of my willingness to engage in such lopsided matches? Is this the sort of battle a noble person seeks?

There are days when I have strong doubts. Just before I left on the trip, I went to my Upper East Side club to play $5-$10 no-limit. It was a tough game, with some very good players. But there were three fish to feed the rest of us. Two of these lost their $800 and $1,000 and left, and I didn't think much about their donations. There was also a woman at the table. She was almost forty and showed a mannish disregard for her appearance. Her shoulder-length hair was wiry and unkempt, and she wore no makeup or jewelry of any kind. And she was awful, a truly horrible poker player. She bought in for $800 and lost that promptly after moving all-in with pocket 5s on the turn against two players with an Ace and a Queen on board. She had enough cash to buy in again, and she promptly lost that. Then she headed out and asked that her seat be held. While she was gone, a pudgy Staten Islander who spoke with an endearingly thick accent said, "What the hell is she doing? She's at the wrong table for that kinda shit."

He was right. She clearly wasn't enough of a player to have developed a deep bankroll. We all sensed that the $2,000 she'd dropped was more than she could comfortably lose. The pain that she showed when she lost a big pot was more profound than the tilty anger that accompanies a tough hand. The loss hurt.

Forty-five minutes later she returned with a wad of twenties, probably gathered from a variety of ATMs. I took that buy-in from her when my two-pair crushed her top pair, weak kicker. She then produced a personal check. Another player at the club, who I could only assume knew her in other walks of life, cashed it. That thousand quickly disappeared. It was a pathetic sight. She was dumbstruck and ashen. I imagined she was contemplating the effects the night's $5,000 setback would have on her life—the bills that would need to be put off, the time it would take to recover.

But I didn't leave that table until she got up and headed out the door. If she had found a way to come up with another buy-in I would have stayed.

California has a bizarre and muddled history with legalized poker. The governing law, which was crafted in the latter half of the nineteenth century, listed many forms of gambling that were explicitly forbidden. Before 1991, Section 330 of the Penal Code read:

"Every person who deals, plays or carries on, opens, or causes to be opened, or who conducts, either as owner or employee, whether for hire or not, any game of faro, monte, roulette, lansquenet, rouge et noire, rondo, tan, fan-tan, stud-horse poker, twenty-one, hokeypoker, or any banking or percentage game played with cards, dice, or any device, for money, checks, credit, or other representative of value . . . is guilty of a misdemeanor. . . ."

According to the law, gaming activities not included in the list could be played legally if local jurisdictions opted to license clubs for such a purpose.

Seeing a hole in the statute, some crafty, shady, and well-connected businessmen were able to obtain licenses for poker clubs in localities in the Los Angeles area in the 1940s. The clubs offered only draw poker—no stud-horse—and claimed to be operating within the limits of the law. Concerned local groups appealed to the state's attorney general, Ulysses Webb, to shut down the clubs. But Webb demurred, determining that while "stud-horse poker" was clearly illegal, there was nothing on the books to forbid draw poker.

Some sources claim that Webb found poker was a permitted activity because he determined it was a game of skill, as opposed to other forms of gambling that were governed strictly by chance. Many in the poker world take Webb's supposed proclamation as an official, legal validation of their pastime. I could find no original sources that confirmed that Webb, or anyone else in California, ever made such a determination. Webb had only one question to tackle: Was draw poker covered by the prohibition of stud-horse poker?

After Webb's ruling, localities in need of tax revenue licensed card rooms all around California, and for years they offered only draw poker variants. But in the 1980s, when hold 'em and 7-stud began to dominate player's attention in Vegas and Atlantic City, restless card room owners began to ask what "stud-horse" poker was exactly. The rules of the game were lost to history. But did the law truly intend to outlaw games like hold 'em and 7-stud? Poker clubs went to court, and thanks largely to the research of gambling law expert I. Nelson Rose, the courts found in *Tibbets v. Van de Kamp* (Nora Tibbets was the owner of the Oaks Card Room and John Van de Kamp the attorney general) that stud-horse poker was a game that was played against the house and was therefore decidedly different from Texas hold 'em. A series of appeals followed, but the ruling was upheld. In 1991, the California legislature amended Penal Code 330 by eliminating stud-horse poker from its list of forbidden games.

More card rooms—many calling themselves casinos—were built. But they were unlike casinos in Vegas and Atlantic City, where operators could offer games like blackjack or craps, which pitted players against the house. California law still forbade "banking or percentage games." Casinos in California made their money either by raking pots or by charging a set rate for a seat at a gaming table. Without the massive profit potential of Vegas-style casinos, California's rooms adopted a more subdued aesthetic. At the time of my trip, they offered none of the glitz or opulence many expect from a gambling hall. The card rooms around San Francisco are so unassuming, in fact, that I imagine most of the local population is completely unaware of the gambling spots in their midst.

Lucky Chances Casino, for example, was set in Colma, a cemetery town just south of San Francisco. The structure was gray and boxy and lacked any sort of glittery signage. When I drove there after the bowling alley birthday bash, I noticed that from the parking lot I could look out on rows of headstones in the Italian Cemetery across the street. The interior was equally unassuming. A small lobby led to a massive room bisected by an elevated walkway. On one side, poker tables, about twenty-five in all, were lined up tightly together. The space was scrupulously clean, with a busy staff of waitresses and busboys delivering and disposing of food.

On the other side of the walkway, a space of equal size was jammed with semicircular tables and packed with people of Chinese ancestry who were playing pai gao. On my first trips to California casinos, I was enthralled by the action at the pai gao tables. I watched, trying to determine the game's rules. The game seemed to start when a dealer distributed a deck into seven equal piles. Then a small stainless steel plate that was covered by a cup was handed to one of the players. That player would proceed to slam the cup-plate assembly on the table anywhere from two to seven times. The cup would then be removed to reveal a die. The piles of cards were then distributed. Each player would divide his own cards into two piles. The cards were then revealed. A Chinese man would inevitably scream "Hee-ya," and large chunks of money would be moved around the table. I had no idea why.*

---

\* I've since learned that the rules of pai gao are extraordinarily simple. One player serves as the bank and plays against all other players. Seven cards are given to each player. The players must then divide their cards into two poker hands, one with five cards, the other with two. The five-card hand must be of greater value than the two-card hand. When the cards are revealed, each player compares his hands to the bank's hands. If both of the player's hands are superior to the bank's, then the player wins the amount he bet. If only one of his hands is better, neither the player nor the bank wins. If both of the bank's hands are superior, the bank takes the player's bet. The die simply determines where the dealer starts distributing the piles of cards.

But at Lucky Chances I had no use for pai gao and headed directly for the poker sign-up board. I was shocked at the stakes available: $3-$6, $6-$12, and $9-$18 limit, along with $1-$2 and $2-$5 no-limit. I asked to have my name put on the $2-$5 list, but there were twenty names before mine, and it appeared they had only one table of $2-$5 running. I asked if they might start another game, but was told that every table they had was in use. I resigned myself to a long wait and ordered some of the surprisingly good Chinese food they offered. But after an hour, only one name was called off the list. I could wait another three hours or more before they called my name. I decided to try some of the other local card rooms.

I returned to Artichoke Joe's, where I'd played my first casino poker years earlier. I had a brief upwelling of nostalgia as I remembered my first wary steps into the strange space. I remembered the patience and kindness of dealers and other players when I tried to figure out the rules of hold 'em. ("Blinds? I don't get it?") But the games at Artichoke Joe's were even smaller—topping out at $6-$12. I couldn't waste my time with that. There was only one major card room in the Bay Area remaining, Bay 101 in San Jose. But Bay 101 offered no big-bet games at all—only limit.

Until this trip, I had thought of San Francisco as having an endless supply of games at every imaginable stake. That's the way it seemed when I was playing $3-$6 limit while in the area. I had progressed to the point where there was only one table in all of the Bay Area that held even the slightest interest for me. I'd come a long way.

Even if I were to adhere to conventional wisdom and say that fish hunting presented no ethical problems, I'd still have reason to worry about my devotion to the game. When I looked back at some episodes that took place during the trip and over the previous years, I couldn't help but acknowledge some of the uglier aspects of my personality.

I'd been tilty, unable to let reason dictate my actions after encountering adversity. I'd been petulant, cursing a total stranger who had done nothing but attempt to outplay me. I'd been bored and frustrated and condescending and aloof.

But there was no outward evidence of my most troubling mental state. When I played against a particularly inept opponent, like Rick, the loser in New Orleans, I became vicious. I had no concern with good-natured competition or intellectual gamesmanship. I didn't want simply to *win* or *outplay* him. He wasn't my peer; he was my prey, my enfeebled, hemorrhaging prey. I yearned to dismember him. When I wiped Rick out, I felt a frighteningly intense and primal satisfaction.

I don't think Robert could have guessed I was capable of this sort of thought when he spoke of my "inclination" for the game. But if these failings were what he had in mind, I wouldn't argue with any disgust he expressed.

# SAN DIEGO

**I** LEFT SAN FRANCISCO, A CITY I LOVE, AFTER ONLY TWO nights, without seeing many friends or eating in my favorite restaurants. Most remarkably, I failed to find time for Ebisu, the best sushi restaurant I know of. The yellowtail alone would make a long, inconvenient detour worthwhile. But I had less than two weeks left in the trip, and I needed to find the best games I could in those few days. My bankroll was in good shape. With continued online success and the fortunate week in Vegas, I was up more than $17,000 for the trip. Still, I had to be prepared to lose as much as $5,000 in a single hand at Commerce, so anything I could add to my bankroll before I played the big game would be helpful.

I was headed to the San Diego area. My father lived in Coronado, an idyllic island town just a short bridge crossing away from the city. For that stop on the trip I'd have all the restful comforts of home (actually, far more comforts than could be found in my Brooklyn apartment). I very much looked forward to strolls on the beach and dinners with familial company.

My father was an avid cardplayer. He flirted with card counting in blackjack, played competitive contract bridge, and for most of his life has been involved in home poker games. For more than fifteen years he attended a Wednesday night game for stakes that were trivial to the doctors and entrepreneurs who came week after week; the big winner might take home an extra $100. After a number of years, he grew close to many of the players. But, as my father told it, there was dissension. One of the game's original members was an officious bully who arbitrarily devised rules of conduct that he sought to impose. The man's relationships with some players were so adversarial that my father and other, calmer players were forced to intervene in the occasional conflict. Then, one day, my father got a call from the self-appointed group leader. He told my father that he had unilaterally decided to ban another player from the game. My father didn't object. He quit the game. Years ago, when he told me about this conflict and the outcome, he was still upset. "I saw these people every week for fifteen years," he told me. It was a loss.

Before long he and some other players broke off and found their way to another game with similar stakes. This one had a more stable mix of personalities, and at the time of my visit, the game had been going smoothly for many years.

My parents divorced when I was very young, so my father and I spent little time together during my formative years. In my adult life, we had periods when we communicated horribly, perhaps because we never learned how to chat—shoot the shit. Conversations seemed burdened with expectation, as if we had to focus on issues with some gravity. When things went poorly, our discussions could be labored or uncomfortable. But in recent years, our love of cards has given us an easy avenue for enjoyable conversation. By not having to search for topics of common interest, there is less pressure, and our time together is easier, more enjoyable. Our dialogue may not have the tear-jerking power of Ray Kinsella's final words in *Field of Dreams* ("Hey, Dad . . . you wanna have a catch?"), but there is a poignancy to seeing my father concentrate mightily as I describe a hand and ask, "Wait, so what was the turn?"

San Diego was said to have a busy poker scene, with several active card clubs and a few Indian casinos within driving distance. My first night in town, I headed to the closest card room to Coronado, the Village Club in Chula Vista, which I was told had a $5-$10 no-limit game.

The Village Club sat on a commercial strip, beside gas stations, 7-Elevens, and automotive repair shops. Large chunks of the gold-paint lettering on the club's sign had peeled away. Once inside the club, I was shocked by the size of the space: seven tables in all. It was the smallest legal poker room I'd ever seen. It was also the dingiest. The chairs were beaten, the tan walls lacked any sort of decoration, and the thin industrial carpet was marred with huge black spots. It smelled of sweat and oily Chinese food. This place, I thought, couldn't survive in the underground New York scene. It would be too nasty even for the degenerates who populated the Fourteenth Street club.

Within five minutes of my arrival, an argument started at a $2-$4 limit table. A Chinese man and woman, both middle-aged, screamed full-throat at each other over some perceived breach of etiquette. The argument probably would have gone more smoothly in Mandarin or maybe Cantonese, if indeed they shared one of these dialects, but it was conducted in fractured, article-less English that the other players found hysterical. Almost everyone in the club gathered around the table to laugh at the spectacle. It was several minutes before the security guards—huge men, who would be able bouncers in a biker bar—settled the seething patrons down.

The list for the $5-$10 game was formidable, with nine names ahead of mine. I couldn't bear the idea of idle times in these grim surroundings, so I asked to sit in the $8-$16 Omaha high-low game that was under way and had an open seat.

I sat next to a short, stocky tattooed young man who glowered at me.

"You here to take my money, too?" he asked, his tone menacing.

I smiled and gave a what–are–you–gonna–do shrug and turned away.

"Everybody thinks they can take my fucking money tonight." I was looking away, so I couldn't tell if the comment was addressed to me.

In casino high–low split games, rules demand that in order to take half of the pot the best low hand can have no card higher than 8. So if the best low is a 9-high, there will be no split pot—the high hand will scoop, take the entire pot. In Omaha high–low, the players know there will only be a split pot if three of the five community cards are below 8. On a flop of Q-J-T, for instance, anyone hoping for a low can safely abandon the hand.

I had played very little Omaha high–low, and was unclear on some of the mathematical issues and finer points of strategy. I knew the one basic rule of high–low split games: Don't draw to half the pot. In these games, the key is to scoop entire pots. Those who pay to see cards that will award them only one half of the winnings are bound to do poorly in the long run. But the players who frequent high–low split games love to draw—it's why they're there, because every single preflop hand seems to have reasonable potential.

And in the Village Club game, there seemed to be a pull beyond statistics or even a wild hope that made the players throw bets into pots. Many seemed to view folding—at any time, on any street—as a moral or constitutional failure. I could find no other explanation for the action I witnessed or the cards that were revealed. In one hand I held A♠-K♥-2♦-6♠, and the board was J♠-8♦-4♠-9♣-7♠. I had the Ace-high flush, the nut high, and A-2-4-7-8, the nut low, yet I was not just called by two other players on the river—the angry tattooed man to my left raised me. I, of course, raised back, then he raised again. The third player in the hand kept calling. When we finally showed our hands, I revealed mine and the other two players simply threw their cards in the muck. I figured I'd be splitting the low half of the pot with someone else who had A-2 amongst their hole cards. But no.

"Good hand," my ornery tablemate said, though clearly he didn't mean it.

"Thank you," I said softly as I started to pile a mound of chips so vast that they were spilling into my neighbor's space.

"I'll buy you a beer," he said.

"I'm good, thanks."

"No, I'll buy you a beer." His tone frightened me.

"Thank you. That's very nice."

The beer came and I toasted him. I then subtly angled my chair so that my gaze would naturally point in the opposite direction.

I was fortunate to find good cards that night, scooped a couple of pots, and left with another $800 padding my bankroll.

The small parking lot at the Village Club was full when I arrived earlier that night. They had an option for valet parking, but I hated paying $2 for parking when a short walk was completely free. When I left the club, the spot that I found half a block away felt horribly distant. I half-jogged to my car, taking the occasional backward glance to ensure that my beer-buying friend hadn't taken a path behind me. If I came back to this dump, I thought, I'd use the valet. A can of Mace might also be in order.

I did return the following night. And once again, the evening began with yelling. A player at the $5-$10 no-limit hold 'em table at which I was playing insisted that the dealer had failed to correctly divide a previous pot that was contested by three players. I missed the hand, and so had no opinion, but his arguing brought the action to a halt. He demanded that the floor manager pull the surveillance tape and review the hand. She refused, but he persisted, offering a series of insults and demands until she finally relented. She disappeared for fifteen minutes then returned to declare that the pot, in fact, had been split properly.

"It's good. He did it right," she barked. The discussion was over.

He seemed satisfied, but I doubted that her absence was evidence of any effort. I guessed she'd taken a lengthy smoke break.

The game that night was good, but my tolerance for the environment was short. An additional odor had been added to the near-toxic mix—ammonia. An emergency cleanup was required in the bathroom, and the response had left the club air unbreathable. Two hours and a few hundred in profit was all I could manage that night.

My father has been something of a gambler in his life. He twice left stable moorings to start retail businesses that he felt had value. Both times, he properly weighed risk against potential reward and did extremely well. When I e-mailed to ask him about his feelings about my dealings in poker, I expected a sympathetic reply. Here, in part, is what he wrote:

> *I became and remain concerned that you might be addicted to the game. I am also concerned that at some point your relationship with Marisa might suffer significantly. The idea that you might play for enough money to put all your assets in jeopardy has also entered my mind.*
>
> *But I think you have several things going for you as a professional. You're smart, you seem to have the ability to play the hand whatever the outcome of the last hand might have been. Your history suggests to me that you have a chance at becoming successful, as you have looked at many things in your career and even when nothing came of an idea you retained the ability to look ahead.*

I would have expected my mother, a poet, to have greater trepidations. When I asked her to commit some thoughts to the keyboard, she responded with all the speed and thoroughness I expected:

*Am I concerned about your evolution into a professional poker player? You bet I am. Not a gambler myself, I have an intense distrust of any activity that has the potential to become addictive (or compulsive). I'm also concerned that you are no longer in a field that is secure in terms of earning a steady income. . . . Poker is hot right now, a fad in America. We all know what happens to fads. If this trend plays itself out, will you have another career to fall back on? . . .*

*With it all, you look happier to me than ever before in your adult life. Much of this is due to your relationship with Marisa, but I firmly believe that career satisfaction is imperative to a feeling of contentment, so I thank poker, especially Texas hold 'em, for its contribution to your exhilaration with life.*

And what about Marisa, the person this avocation would affect most directly? She has had and will continue to have opportunities to express reservations, concerns, or dismay. If and when they are expressed I will heed them. But for the time being I have no reason to assume she has anything but complete faith in my judgment and ability.

On my last day in San Diego, I went to Ocean's Eleven Casino in Oceanside, about forty-five minutes north of the city. It was a large card space, in many ways similar to Lucky Chances, with a large room of Chinese men playing pai gao and an equally large room with medium- and low-stakes poker. Their biggest no-limit game was $5-$5 with a $500 maximum buy-in. I was able to get a seat after a short wait.

For the first half hour I didn't play a hand as I assessed the other players. No one seemed especially talented or skilled, and there were clearly a few weak spots. The player to my left, portly and in his midforties, was calling far too frequently. From the searching expression he wore most of the time, I guessed that his forward-moving chips were expressions of blind hope: *Who knows?* I could almost hear him thinking. *Maybe I'll hit a King.* In the three-seat, directly across the table, was a rail-thin Chinese man with unkempt greasy hair and an unlit cigarette dangling from his mouth. He spent at least half of his time away from the table, showing far more interest in pai gao. He returned to the table only after another player complained about the continually empty seat.

Soon after he returned, I was on the button and held A♠-9♥. The Chinese man, in early position, limped, and all folded to me. I opted to raise, apply some pressure with a decent hand and favorable position. The calling station was in the small blind, and he called. The Chinese man called as well.

The flop came: A♦-8♥-4♦.

I had top pair, mediocre kicker. The two players checked to me and I bet $45. The small blind called, and the Chinese man instantly raised all-in. It would cost me another $140 to call.

This action dictated a fold. This man check-raised into two players—an immense show of strength. But I paused, not willing to immediately release this hand. I wanted to think it over.

I'd played Chinese gamblers before—guys interested in games like pai gao—and have found them to be extraordinarily aggressive—capable of raising on all sorts of hands. Racial profiling of this sort may be distasteful, but experience with similar players was all I had to work with.

If this guy fit the stereotype, I had to wonder what hand he could be playing that would have me beat. A-T, A-J, A-Q? That didn't make any sense. He'd raise with those hands. Pocket 4s? Maybe. But that was the only hand I could think of that made sense in the situation and could beat me. In the entire deck of cards there was only one hand he could have that would beat the one I held. I concluded that the chances he held a lesser hand were great enough to make this hand worth playing. But what to do about the calling station? He was almost certainly on a flush draw, and I wanted him out of the pot, or at least to make it very expensive for him to play.

"All-in," I announced and pushed my remaining $400 into the pot.

The calling station paused for a second, shrugged, then pushed his money forward.

The turn: 2♣, and the river, 2♠.

The Chinese man showed A-7, and the other player, K♦-6♦, for the flush draw.

A quick strike and I was up $600.

Just twenty minutes later, I was once again on the button and once again there was one limper in the pot. But the limper in this case was fortyish and seemed to play a by-the-numbers sort of game. I thought he was someone who could be pushed off a pot if I showed strength, so with my 9♥-T♠, I took an aggressive posture and raised to $20. The big blind and limper called.

The flop was a bonanza: 9♣-T♦-5♥. I had top two-pair.

My opponent bet $75, and I didn't want to play around, as there were a number of straight draws on board. I raised to $225. The blind folded, and the fortyish man stopped, seeming very concerned about my play. After a full minute of thought, he called.

The turn: Q♥.

My opponent instantly announced all-in and slid his $625 in chips forward.

I preemptively apologized to the table. "Sorry, guys, this one's going to take a few minutes." They nodded, appreciating that this was a big decision.

What hands made sense? Q-T? Did he just nail his own superior two-pair? Possible. But if he did nail a huge hand like that, why would he make such a massive bet, one that seemed designed to chase me from the pot? If he hit two-pair, he could have either bet $350 or maybe tried for a check-raise. I couldn't square top two with what I was seeing. A set? That was even less likely. This hesitation on the flop looked genuine to me, and if he had a set, his money would have hit the pot much faster.

What about a draw, something like Q-J? That might explain

the hesitancy on the flop. He wasn't sure if he wanted to call such a big bet on nothing more than a draw. And when the Queen hit on the turn, he would have made top pair along with his draw. If that were the case, he might be trying to buy the pot with a hand that had, at the very least, a ton of potential. The bet, from his view, might be enough to put me off of pocket Kings. And if I called, he still had plenty of outs. There were other possible draws. He could have picked up a straight and flush draw on the turn. In the end, I couldn't pinpoint a specific hand. But I thought he was on a draw and I figured that I was still a statistical favorite.

I called.

The dealer placed the river, the 6♣, on the board. My opponent immediately declared, "You're good," before he even saw my hand, and threw his cards in the muck. I'll never know what he had, but my decision was clearly correct.


That evening I went to dinner with my father, stepmother Diana, and a couple they're friendly with. I arrived late, having been delayed by some traffic and a wrong turn. When I sat and ordered, my father asked how my session had gone, and I told him that it had gone well. He pressed for details, so I set about describing the session's key hands in a way that the nonplayers would understand. All listened intently and interjected questions when they didn't understand a point. My energy was high, as remnants of adrenaline were still in my system, and I felt particularly lucid as I described the key issues I considered in each determinative situation. As I spoke, I looked at their faces. My father's small smile revealed an intense pride. The rest were rapt, hanging on my descriptions and explanations with a fascination that momentarily surprised me.

After the meal I thought about the attention my story was given and wondered if poker was an innately interesting subject or if I just happened to be a good raconteur that night. After some consideration, I decided that neither of these elements explained the dynamic especially well. The story I had told, like all good stories, held the listeners' attention because of the quality of the detail. I was able to parse the situation and highlight each of the compelling aspects and show how all of these factors influenced my final action.

I was only able to do this, I came to think, because somewhere during the trip, my awareness had improved. Having played an untold number of hands in the previous months, my capacity for breaking down a poker situation into its elemental parts had reached a new level. I had discovered a new level of clarity.

If, earlier in my trip, I had harbored doubts about my ability to compete effectively with the others at the Commerce game, they all but vanished with this discovery. I had made my $20,000 and I was playing great poker. I was ready for Los Angeles. Ready for Commerce.

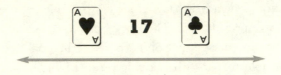

# 17

# LOS ANGELES

I LEFT SAN DIEGO FOR THE SHORT DRIVE TO LOS ANGELES with nearly two weeks remaining in my trip. I wanted to make sure that I had ample time to experience the breadth of the L.A. poker scene. Beyond the Commerce Casino, where I'd finally play the $10-$20 no-limit, there were a variety of massive poker halls worthy of a visit: the Bicycle Club, Hollywood Park, the Hustler Casino, to name just a few. But before I hit any of those spots, I decided to stop by Commerce. With the World Poker Tour's Los Angeles Poker Classic in full swing, I wanted to get a view of the action.

I arrived on a Wednesday, late afternoon, and moved through Commerce's massive ground floor. I entered the lower-limit area, where every one of the hundred-fifty-plus tables was filled. Four sign-up boards spread throughout the space were active, and the drone of floor managers calling players to their seats blared over the general murmur. I moved through to the high-limit side— the spot where I'd be playing $10-$20—and at least half of the sixty tables were filled, and they were opening games continually. Did I want a $400-$800 seat? one of the floor men asked. No, thanks.

I proceeded past a faux-marble statue of an enraged stallion and went up a flight of stairs to the tournament area. In that room there were another sixty tables. At one end of the room, a tournament was in progress—a small one, with roughly one hundred people playing 7-stud. On the right side of the room about fifteen tables were running satellites, the single-table tournaments that players use to win their way into larger, more expensive events. The $10,000 buy-in main event of the LAPC would start the following week, and Commerce was running satellites for the event twelve hours a day. I decided to take a shot: A million-dollar win and a TV appearance would be good for book sales, I figured. And I liked the way I was playing.

When they started a $100 satellite, I played and quickly lost. Soon after I entered a supersatellite—a multitable tournament whose sole purpose was to send a few players to the main event. It was a $200 rebuy affair, and I managed to dump $800 into that in less than an hour's play.

I left the Commerce that evening $1,000 lighter. I'd offered a small donation to those who would cash in the on LAPC's main event. With 30 percent of the total prize pool going to the first-place finisher, $300 of the eventual winner's $1 million–plus take would be money that was once mine.

I smiled as I thought about this small offering and my role in delivering it. I was a conduit of sorts, a mechanism for transferring money from the most helpless, the fishiest, to the most able and richest. I'd traveled the country, taking money from those who were out of their depth when playing me, and served a portion of it to others with even greater ability. Because of people like me, money found it's way from the small-stakes fish to the pockets of Daniel Negreanu and Phil Ivey.

The poker world, I came to think, is like a giant inverted pyramid, where the most skilled and richest reside at the bottom, the narrowest part of the structure. The wide opening at the top is where the vast numbers of fish play. At every downward step, there are fewer people of greater skill. The entire structure is continually shaken, spilling money from the pockets of those at the top. It falls, and the players directly below hold out their hands to catch whatever they can. But those in the middle can't manage to hold on to everything that falls before them, and much travels down the narrowing walls to the very bottom where the likes of Doyle Brunson, Barry Greenstein, and Chip Reese claim every spare dollar.

When I visualized this structure, my thoughts turned to my placement within it. I clearly fit in the lowest 10 percent, maybe a good deal lower. As well as I'd been playing, perhaps I was in the top one percent and could play competitively with world-class pros. The key point was this: I was better than most, but clearly not as good as others. That was all I needed to know.

As I thought about it, I found another feature of this pyramid more striking: its isolation. The money came in through the top, where people from all lines of work contributed. Here the poker economy interacted with the larger economy, taking in whatever it could. But by the time the money moved past the first level, it only moved downward, never upward or outward.

Though I'm no economist, I have a basic understanding of how wealth is created and how money moves in societies. To put it simply, in almost every sector of the economy, when a class of products flourishes, the greater demand for it benefits just about everyone. The manufacturers and marketers get rich. If capitalism is operating as it should, the workers will benefit from greater job security or higher wages. When things are going really well in a specific area, the economy as a whole benefits from the increased wealth, as everyone has a little more to spend.

But the poker economy manufactures nothing—no technology or wisdom that improves lives. With the exception of the few people who win, nobody's lifestyle is improved. Any benefit the pros and semipros see from the boom is theirs and theirs alone.

The fish who feed us all see no gain whatsoever. And we offer nothing to the greater wealth of the country or the world.

We take. It's what we do.

Hollywood Park Casino is in Inglewood, just a couple of minutes from the L.A. Forum, where the Lakers used to play. It's a rough neighborhood, one of the highest-crime areas in Los Angeles. But the interior of the casino does not reflect the dangerous surroundings. Like Commerce, Hollywood Park is big and clean and well run. The high-limit area is small, holding only ten tables. But the casino is easily accessible from the 405 and 10 freeways and draws sizable crowds to its dozens of low-limit games.

The only big-bet game in the high-limit area was $5-$10 pot-limit hold 'em. And soon after arriving on my second night in L.A., a seat opened. I pulled $1,000 from my pocket, which looked to be about the table average. After two hours in which I found some good cards, I worked my stack up to $1,700. It looked like my hot streak was continuing. The players at that table had some skill, but the competition wasn't especially troublesome. I usually had a pretty good idea of where I stood.

Then, while in the big blind, I found Q-8, a lousy hand by anyone's estimation. But it was limped to me, so I had no opportunity to fold before the flop came down 9♦-T♦-J♠. I flopped a straight, the second nuts. There were four players in this pot, and with two diamonds on board, I couldn't risk giving a free card. I bet out $40. A raise came from my left: $120 to play. Then a player in late position announced, "Pot." He was reraising. The total bet: $460.

I didn't love the spot. A raise and a reraise after my bet indicated great strength, and either of the other two players could have K-Q. But top two, a set, or even 8-9 for the sucker straight, were possibilities. When I looked at the board and considered the vast number of possible holdings, I couldn't see folding. My $1,700 was soon in the pot. I nodded when I saw the late position's K-Q. I offered a "Nice hand" as the $4,000 pot was pushed toward him.

I had lost my biggest pot of the trip. But this cold deck caused me no consternation, no difficulty at all. I reviewed the situation with a few at the table and decided that although a huge laydown was a possible course, my decision was reasonable. I lost, and with my larger bankroll, I was more than able to handle that sort of hit. With a bit of pride, I realized I didn't feel even the slightest hint of tilt. I pulled another $1,200 from my pocket and settled in for the next hand.

A few minutes later, a fifty-year-old wearing dress slacks and a sporty silk shirt and showing a head of perfectly coiffed gray hair came into the room. With a wide smile, he pumped the floor manager's hand, then traded a joke with a waitress. This guy was clearly a regular.

"Yuri," he said, as he offered me his hand. He then professed his love for the dealer and the others at the table; all smiled. Yuri made a threat to greet a large dour-looking man with a kiss. The man offered a warning in reply: "You better not, Yuri. It's going to be some serious shit if you do," a small smile peeking from the corners of his mouth. Unbowed, Yuri followed though on his threat, forcefully placing his hand on one side of the man's great head and lowering his lips to the opposite cheek. Everyone guffawed.

Yuri sat and pulled a bank-wrapped $10,000 bundle from his pocket; he placed $3,000 on the felt.

Yuri raised each of the first six hands, and bet each of the first six flops, taking most of the small pots in the process. This guy was here to spread his money around, I thought. I started praying for a big hand.

With Yuri immediately to my left, I found pocket Queens under the gun. I limped, deciding that Yuri would do the raising for me, and he did: $50 to go. There were two callers, and when it was back to me, I announced, "Raise the pot," for a total bet of

$260. Yuri called, as I knew he would, and everyone else got out of my way. The flop came Q♠-7♠-2♦. I had a set of Queens, the nuts. There was a potential spade draw on board but I wasn't about to worry about that. I was proceeding as if I had a mortal lock on the hand, and my only concern was getting every dollar out of Yuri I could. Should I check, slow-play? No, I decided. Yuri had shown a willingness to call bets with next to nothing, so I decided to bet and hope he'd have enough to call me down. "Two-fifty," I said. The bet was met with an instant call. Beautiful. Yuri had something. The turn brought a 4, and I bet out $400. Call. The river brought a King, and I announced I was all-in for my last $300. Yuri called again, this time with some eagerness. I showed my set and he nodded approvingly. Yuri then said that he, too, had a set, 2s.

"Ah," I replied, acknowledging the tough spot he was in. But I didn't believe it for a second. Yuri had a King in his hand. Probably nothing better than K-T or K-J. With Yuri's help I was even for the night.

Yuri then claimed he was upset with me and was changing seats. He moved from my immediate left to my immediate right, which was fine with me. I was thrilled to have position on this maniac.

But my cards went sour for a short time, and I had little to do but watch Yuri's antics. In his new seat Yuri was sitting to the immediate left of a twenty-something, Marc, who'd clearly spent some time with the Grateful Dead, or would have, had Jerry not died before he reached college. Phish was a more likely outlet for his time, I decided. He wore a thick black beard and a knit cap. He was affable enough, and chatted with most everyone at the table, including Yuri and me. He had a nice stack in front of him, close to $3,000, but it didn't take long to see that the arsenal in front of him was more deterrent than offensive. He was cautious and, I thought, unlikely to make a big call or a spectacular bluff.

Yuri seemed to have come to the same conclusion. After a half hour or so of sitting to Marc's left, Yuri raised under the gun to

$40. There was a late-position caller and Marc called from the big blind—but he didn't look especially happy about his action. The flop came A♥-K♠-8♥. Yuri then tipped up his cards so that I could see them: pocket Tens. This was about as bad a flop for pocket Tens as I could imagine. But after Marc checked, Yuri bet the pot—$130. The late-position player folded and Marc thought hard, looking at the board with great suspicion before calling. The turn was the 6♠, and once again Marc checked and, predictably, Yuri bet the pot, $390. Marc seemed to be in need of a Pepcid. Once again, he called. The river was a stunning card: the K♥. If one of the two was chasing a flush, he got there. If someone had second pair, he now had trips.

Disgusted, Marc checked, and Yuri counted out $700. Marc shook his head and showed A-Q, then folded. Yuri then flashed his Tens. Marc was livid. He got up and walked in small circles in the area around his seat.

"Here, take it," Yuri announced. He was pushing a stack of twenty green chips, $500, to Marc.

"What?" Marc asked.

"That was not nice. Here, take the money!" he insisted.

Marc didn't protest.

Over the next twenty minutes Yuri continued to badger the table. He raised consistently and in one hand found four callers, including Marc. On a flop of 5-6-8, Yuri was the aggressor, betting the $200 pot. Marc was having none of it this time and called defiantly. The turn brought a 4. Now if either player held a 7, he made the straight. When checked to, Yuri bet again: $600. Marc called. A Jack on the river brought another check from Marc, and another pot-sized bet from Yuri: $1,800. Marc called in a shot. Yuri showed J-7, for the straight. Marc, disgusted, threw his cards into the muck. This time there were no refunds.

I left soon after this hand, having managed a few hundred in profit.

*Poker: a tough way to make an easy living. Beats the hell out of working.
I just love cards.* Careerists or aspiring poker careerists throw out
these phrases like they provide an explanation as to why they've
opted for this avocation over some more typical profession. After
two years of semiprofessional play and three months of an all-
consuming road trip, I'd come to look at these explanations as
ridiculous.

First off, there's nothing remotely easy about this line of work.
A $100,000 annual salary comes by way of massive gains and
gut-wrenching losses. The hours are horrendous. Something like
7:00 P.M. to 6:00 A.M. would be the most profitable shift, a schedule sure to isolate oneself from those who don't inhabit the
poker universe.

Those who do inhabit this world include the unclean, the
nasty, the tilting, the self-absorbed whiners, to name just a few, all-
in-all, a fairly grim collection of personalities. What's worse is that
when I read my own accounts of episodes from the trip, I realize
that I, at various points, have exhibited all the characteristics I
truly despise. I tilted, I whined, I snapped. Like everyone else
around this game, I've been stripped down to my most loathsome
traits. There's nothing remotely easy about that.

Is this life in any way superior to a regular job? Yes, jobs often suck. We're all aware of that. But the truth is that I'm cre-
ative and highly qualified for any number of jobs that would
provide a satisfactory income. I'm not at a place in my life
where I need to settle for days and weeks and years of tedium.
Between my writing, programming, and project management
skills, I'd find something that suited my skills and need for cre-
ative outlet. I've had rewarding work experiences before. I can
have them again.

What about my love of the game? Yes, there are moments

when I find poker more satisfying than anything I've ever done. I'm probably better at poker than anything I've ever taken an interest in. I wonder if it is one of the few things in this world for which I might one day be considered a true great. But past interests for which I didn't have nearly that acuity—writing, basketball, skiing, filmmaking—never left me addled and frightened. I never agonized over a looming bankruptcy or considered the activity inherently unfair. None of these activities required me to keep fifty grand in cash on hand so I could grind out a living.

So what would be my quip, my standard line, when someone asked me why I chose poker over all the other things the world has to offer? I was drawing a blank.

I took another trip to Commerce and dumped another two grand into satellites with no luck. I'd given up on playing in the main event of the LAPC after a nasty beat in a supersatellite, and I headed to the Bicycle Club, which would be my last game before I hit the high limits.

The Bike is yet another of the massive L.A. poker halls that seems to have acres of tables and sign-up boards the size of freeway billboards. I arrived early in the afternoon and wound my way between the active low-limit tables to the high-limit area. A $5-$10 no-limit game would start before long, I was told. In the meantime I could play in the $300 buy-in $2-$5 game.

I sat and played for an hour. Somehow, I'd found some discipline at this lowered buy-in and managed to get through the session without blasting off my chips. When they called me for the $5-$10 no-limit game I was pleased that I'd lost only $50.

The first few hours of this game were uneventful. The play was tight and cautious, and I didn't find many situations I found favorable. My stack saw some minor fluctuations, but nothing distressing or invigorating.

Sometime around 8:00, after I had played for a few hours, a

young woman sat to my left. I glanced over at her a few times and determined that she couldn't possibly be far beyond her twenty-first birthday. She had a delicate complexion, a hooked nose, a shallow chin, and long, stringy brown hair. Yet somehow these independently unattractive characteristics came together in an appealing way. There was a lack of affectation in her appearance I appreciated. She wore no makeup and covered her body with a loose-fitting sweater. She looked nothing like the halter-top and spike-heel-wearing women who accompany many of the top pros. I've never been one for trashy women, and I found the sight of this young woman refreshing.

She wore an iPod, and from the start played with a laudable aggressiveness and tenacity. She bought in for $1,500 and wasn't afraid to put those chips to work. Her bets were large, but precise. On more than one occasion she put opponents in very difficult spots. I was impressed. My estimation of her skills spiked in a hand about two hours into the session. She took a brutal beat, having her Aces cracked by a horrid river card. She responded with a soft "hee-ya," and knocked the table. "Nice hand," she offered to her fishy counterpart and then casually pulled another $1,500 from her roll.

She took the loss like a pro. In fact, I had no doubt: She was a pro.

"I'm Jay," I said, leaning in her direction.

"Jillian," she replied with a soft smile.

"Tough beat," I said.

She shrugged. "Yeah, I guess."

"Are you a pro?" I blurted. "You sure as hell play like one."

"I play some. But I do some other stuff. I have a band." Someone at the table might have been listening, and she didn't want to identify herself as a shark.

She played bass, I learned, and her band played a hybrid of ambient and pop. I didn't know what that might sound like, but replied approvingly anyway. "How long you been playing?"

"A few years. I don't think I'm that good. I still have a ton to learn."

"Think you're going to stick with it?" I asked.

She pointed her eyes toward the ceiling, searching for the answer. In her face I could see the struggle. The session thus far had been brutal to her, and at that moment she couldn't endure the thought of a lifetime of ridiculous beats and shallow conversation.

"Yeah, I know what you mean," I said, before she started her reply.

# 18

# LOS ANGELES, PART II

THE TIME HAD ARRIVED. WITH MY BANKROLL NEARING $40,000 and with just a week left on my trip, it was time to go to the high-limit board at Commerce and have my name put on the $10-$20 no-limit list. I was apprehensive as I drove from my downtown hotel through the maze of freeways that led to my destination. I had to be prepared for a five-figure loss in the next few days. I wasn't about to buy in short, and if I was ready for the move up, I wouldn't play scared. "Ten thousand," I said aloud in the car. "I'm willing to lose ten thousand dollars."

I arrived at the casino at 2:00 P.M. and walked directly to the floor man maintaining the sign-up board for the $10-$20 game. I announced my preference and he replied, "Seat open," and pointed me to a table in the corner. I nodded and strode the short distance to the open seat. Once I was at the table a chip porter appeared by my side. I asked for $500 in chips. The other $2,000 I'd keep in cash, a pile of hundreds that I'd keep propped between my chips and the low cushion that bordered the table. I'd come to love playing with stacks of bills. Taking a handful of hundreds and blithely tossing them toward the pot, I found, was more intimidating than sliding a stack of chips, no matter their denomination.

I sat and surveyed the table. Immediately I was struck by the sizes of some of the stacks. The seven seat couldn't have had much more than $1,000, and two of the other players appeared to have even less. I'd heard that I should be prepared to do battle with players holding stacks in excess of $10,000. What was going on here?

Chances were these guys weren't properly bankrolled. They might be playing scared, which was fine with me. A little extra aggression was in order. So when I saw 6♦-7♦ in middle position, I announced a raise. Four times the big blind would be appropriate, so I took some chips in hand and made four ministacks with four chips each.

"One-sixty," announced the dealer.

Huh? I then glanced at my chips. Each was worth $10, not the $5 I was accustomed to, and I'd just put out a ridiculously large open-raise. But I didn't flinch or grimace. I tried to act as though this was exactly what I intended. It was folded around to the big blind, who happened to have the shortest stack at the table— roughly $600—and he quickly moved all-in. I tossed my cards at the muck, and he flashed pocket Queens. My first hand at the high limits did not reflect my full range of skills.

A few hands later, I was in middle position when the under-the-gun player raised to $100, and he was quickly reraised by the player to my right, who made it $300. I had trash and tossed away my cards. The player to my left then paused, peeked at his cards, and sighed. He motioned for me to lean his way. I did, and he showed me his hand—A♣-Q♥. "I've been having trouble with this hand lately," he said. And I refrained from saying, Of course you have. It's a second-rate hand at best, and with this kind of heat, it should be as easy to fold as 7-2. I mean, what do you think you can beat here? Are you hoping the first raiser had A-J and the second, what, pocket 9s? But this guy, like thousands of other fish, had learned all he knew about hold 'em from the WPT. He knew to wear dark sunglasses and give long dramatic pauses for nearly every decision. But what he missed was that hand valuations in a four-handed, sky-high-blind tournament had no bearing on his current situation.

"All right," he announced. "I'm all-in." And he pushed almost $1,400 forward.

The under-the-gun player folded, but the other player called, showing pocket Kings. The board failed to bring an Ace, and the fish busted.

I was expecting tougher competition, but was well aware that with the World Poker Tour in town, I'd run into a few players who would be playing out of their depth. This guy, I thought, was probably an anomaly. Twenty minutes passed before another notable hand was played. This time the big blind was playing a big pot against a late-position raiser. The late-position player was a solid player, someone I'd decided to steer clear of. The big blind was another sunglasses wearer with a short stack. On the turn, with a board of J-4-9-2, the late-position player had moved in, forcing the big blind to call the last $500 in his stack. The call came so quickly and with such confidence that I was certain the big blind had a set, probably Jacks, the nuts. He showed Q-J, nothing more than top pair, decent kicker. The late-position player showed pocket Aces. But a Queen on the river gave the big blind the pot.

So there were two fish, but I still suspected that I'd be seeing a high proportion of strong players. And when a massive, tattooed man slapped $5,000 on the table and sat to my right, I was genuinely concerned that life might get very difficult. The man had a laptop that he immediately opened. He pulled up a Web site that detailed the negotiations between the NHL franchise owners and the players' union. The previous night *Sports Center* had reported that the hockey season had been officially canceled.

"You involved with hockey?" I asked.

"Yeah."

"Player?"

"Yeah."

"Oh. Tough day."

"Yeah."

I made a mental note: The guy had plenty of money and might have come to the table on a lockout-inspired tilt. I decided to check my theory a little later when hockey man open-raised to $100 in middle position. I had only 6-7, but if this guy was really on tilt, I might bust him if I hit. The flop came T-4-2, a total miss for me. Hockey man bet $75.

Seventy-five into a $200 pot? It looked like a very weak bet to me. If he had a pair, either A-T or Jacks, he'd probably make a better effort to protect his hand. I picked up my pile of bills, counted out three, and tossed them in front of my cards.

"Fine," he said with resignation and threw his cards into the muck.

As I scooped the pot, I thought about what I'd seen thus far: a few fish and a tight-weak hockey pro. Three hours into the night I was up a few hundred, but nothing spectacular. I was playing tighter than I had in some time, as there seemed to be little reason to involve myself in a pot without a great hand. With this table, I thought, I could play like a rock and still get paid if I hit a big hand. But I was bored enough that when I saw A♣-J♣ in middle position, I raised to $80. A late-position player and the big blind, a quiet, older Asian man, called. The flop was a dream: J♦-7♣-4♣. I had top pair, top kicker with a nut-flush draw. When the big blind checked, I bet $200. The late-position player got out of the way, but the big blind called.

The turn brought the A♥. Now I had one of those glorious problems of excess that are so rare in life. My hand was huge—top two with the flush draw—but was in fact so big that I couldn't imagine what cards my opponent could hold that would keep him in this pot. However, I had no interest in nuancing another $300 with craftily small turn and river bets. I wanted his stack, and so I had to hope he was playing some trash like J-7 and hit a bad two-pair. "Five-hundred," I said, reaching into my pile of bills. He called.

The river was the 2♦, a total blank, making the board J♦-7♣-4♣-A♥-2♦.

"All-in," announced the man in the blind.

I gave my head a quick shake. What the hell? Had he been slow-playing a set? If he was, I didn't see I had any choice but to pay him off. I didn't know nearly enough about this guy to consider laying my hand down.

"Call," I said. Immediately, the man tossed his cards toward the muck, without even bothering to see if he might be good at showdown. I showed my hand for all to admire, and as the Asian man left the table, the pot was pushed my way. The pile of yellow, green, and black chips mixed with bills looked like the contents of some glorious piñata. With joy, I picked through my prize and separated the good bits from the spectacular ones.

As I was creating stacks from my mound, one of the better players at the table asked, "What the hell could he have had?" A lousy flush draw was our best guess. The river bet was just a stab of desperation. But even this explanation seemed wanting. I wasn't about to suffer over this mystery. That man had just sent over $2,000 in my direction, and nothing else mattered much.

Things having gone surprisingly well in my first high-limit outing, I decided to play in another tournament, a $1,000 buy-in shootout. The shoot-out structure is one that I love. In a standard tournament, tables start ten-handed, and as players are eliminated, the tournament staff breaks tables and moves players around so that remaining tables stay full. But in a shootout, each starting tensome plays until one person has gathered all of his table's chips. The winners of the initial tables then go on to play each other.

After paying my entry fee, I found my assigned seat, table 34, seat 3. As I walked, I looked around the room. Sean Rice, Mihn Nguyen, Scotty Nguyen, Stan Goldstein, Evelyn Ng, Amir Vahedi, Tony Ma, and countless other pros were wandering about the room as the starting time approached, chatting with one another. When I first played in L.A. a couple of years earlier, I had seen a similar lineup and was starstruck. When Paul Darden and Ron Rose sat at my table, I became so nervous and scared that I was incapable of competing effectively. Mistakes followed, and my exit was quick.

But this time there were no nerves. And when Young Phan, a great tournament pro with spiky black hair sat to my left, I nodded and said hello, feeling no sense of panic. He didn't remove his iPod, but offered a warm smile in reply. A minute later Lee Watkinson, who'd cleared well over $1 million in tournament wins in the previous year, sat to my immediate right. Watkinson's shaved bald head and athletic build gave him a powerful presence. But when I introduced myself, he offered his hand and happily joined in a bit of small talk.

I was sandwiched between two top pros. It took me only a moment to realize that these two, Pham and Watkinson, were now my peers. I, too, was a pro.

Before the trip, I often equivocated when someone asked what I did for a living. I might mention poker along with writing. But I don't think I ever answered, "I play poker," and left it at that. During this three-month stretch my skills and bankroll grew to new, impressive heights. And I made money—a lot of it. That's all it takes to be considered a pro. Sure, I didn't have a face casual players would recognize from televised tournaments, but the fact was that I'd probably clear more on the year than half of those guys. If I wanted to, I could in good conscience drop the "semi" from semipro and leave all pretense of another career behind. *Jay Greenspan, poker pro.* It had a certain ring to it.

Beyond this realization, there was still a lingering question. Over the course of the trip, I thought I improved greatly. I suspected that I was more than an able fish hunter at that point. I thought I could play competitively with some of the best. As the tournament director started the action, I saw how fortunate I was.

With world-class pros on either side of me, I might get an indication that afternoon of just how far my game had come.

In the first hour of the tournament, I mostly assessed my table-mates and played only a few premium hands. There were three fish at the table: a calling station, a maniac, and a player so scared-weak that I had no doubt how his afternoon would go. His stack would dwindle down as he folded everything but true monsters. He'd cling to whatever chips he had as if they held his life force. Likely he'd stick around for a few hours, as he was so cautious that he wouldn't bust early. But without any willingness to gamble, he had almost no chance of accumulating a sizable stack.

A few of the others were skilled. One man I recognized from various stops along the tournament trail. Another, a young well-dressed Asian kid, seemed quite aggressive and took control of the table early on. He raised frequently preflop and was unafraid to commit his chips after the flop, even when he was in hands with Phan and Watkinson. In the first blind level, he hit a big hand and doubled up. But soon he gave most of his chips to Phan on an ill-advised bluff. A short while later, after a quick run of quality cards, Watkinson had developed a nice stack.

The players started to drop, and stacks consolidated. We had started with $1,500 in chips, and by the time we were down to six players, both Phan and Watkinson had over $4,500. My stack had barely grown, and was sitting at $2,200. Then I got lucky. I took pocket Kings against pocket Queens and managed to nearly double my stack and eliminate a player. We were down to five, the two top pros, myself, a calling station, and another decent player.

With the blinds increasing and the table now shorthanded, differences in style became evident. Phan remained tight and cautious. He wasn't panicking and was willing to wait for his spots. Watkinson, however, took an entirely different approach. He usually raised two hands per orbit, and on several occasions he reraised from the blinds. In one particularly interesting hand, the only fish remaining at the table raised from the button, and Watkinson came over the top from the small blind. I folded and waited for the button to make a decision for the remainder of his chips. I considered Watkinson's move. To make his raise, he had taken a stack of chips in one hand and slid them forward with his arm slightly cocked, as if he were partially flexing his biceps. The motion seemed unusual, different somehow. When the button called the reraise, I saw why. Watkinson had a lowly A-3, and he was up against A-J.

Seeing the cards, I was able to put my observation in context. The movement by Watkinson I now knew was a variation on a classic tell; the strong body language and hand motions are evidence of weak cards. Watkinson, who was once a competitive wrestler and maintained a powerful build, was, perhaps subconsciously, attempting to use his presence to intimidate.

About ten hands later, while I had the button, Watkinson again raised. As he moved his chips forward, I thought I spotted the same rigidity in his frame. I then looked at my cards and saw K-4. I announced a reraise. The blinds folded and Watkinson followed, quickly tossing his cards away. I'm not sure if a smile crept on to my lips at that moment, but even if it did, I'd forgive myself that excess. Knowing that I had gained an awareness of my situation that enabled me to pick up on that level of subtlety against that quality of competition showed the depth of my skills.

Another player dropped, and we were down to four: Watkinson, Phan, a fish, and me. With Phan on the button, I found K♣-Q♣, a clear raising hand when playing four-handed. So I raised and Phan called. The flop was 9♣-7♣-4♦. I had two overcards and a flush draw. Upon examining the flop, I decided that I was willing to play this hand for the remainder of my chips. I decided to check and then raise when Phan bet. But Phan checked behind me. The turn brought the T♥, giving me even more ways to make a huge hand, as any Jack would make me a straight. I bet small, a little under half the pot, and Phan raised. I announced all-in, pretty sure I'd be prompting a fold, but Phan called in an instant. He showed a set of 9s. I laid my cards on the table and Phan reacted with disgust. He expected the river to kill him. But instead it was a 4, giving Phan a full house and bouncing me from the tournament.

I played the hand poorly. I never stopped to consider Phan's possible holdings, and didn't give much thought to the caution he'd been displaying. But even so, my mistakes were not egregious. If Phan had anything but a set, I might have gotten him to fold, and had I outs, I very well could have won and put myself in great shape to conquer my table. You need to get lucky on a few occasions to win tournaments, and this was a hand where I very well could have taken an important pot.

I walked out of the tournament room with a welling of pride. I could compete with the likes of Phan and Watkinson. I was sure of it. On any given day, I thought, I can beat anyone.


There are two questions any aspiring pro, including myself, must ask before seriously considering making a career of poker. The first and more obvious of the two is simply this: *Can I beat the games?* These days, with Internet poker providing not only an endless stream of tables but a number of analytical tools that deliver incontrovertible statistics, the answer to this question should never be in doubt. If, after tens of thousands of hands, there is no demonstrable evidence of life-sustaining profit, one can be pretty sure that any attempt to fulfill such ambitions will quickly result in fiscal disaster. If a player consistently shows an ability to garner a livable hourly wage, the second question can be considered.

This question is equally simple, but determining the true answer, I think, is far trickier. The question: *Do I really want to do this?*

As much as I've discussed the difficulties of the poker lifestyle in the course of this book, you might think the answer to this question is determined by one's threshold for pain, that it's a matter of how well one can endure loneliness, losses, and other challenges poker throws a player's way. And for most of the trip this is how I thought. When I was stuck, I endured. When I longed for Marisa's company, I endured. I suffered, and suffering was part and parcel of the game. But at Commerce, I came to think differently.

After my second long session of $10-$20, I saw a small crowd gathering toward one end of the high-limit room. I walked over and saw the reason for the commotion: the *big game* was going. Doyle Brunson, Chip Reese, Gus Hansen, Phil Ivey, and a few others had moved their $4000-$8000 mixed game to Commerce to coincide with the tournament. I settled into a spot where I had an unobstructed view of Phil Ivey.

Ivey was twenty-eight at the time of the LAPC, but he looked younger—twenty-three maybe. Tall, trim, and black, with sharp features and a perfect complexion, Ivey seemed the quintessential young American male. He could fit in anywhere, from a Jay-Z concert to an Old Navy ad. Beyond his looks, Ivey had attributes that could gain him access to some rarefied portions of society.

He is brilliant. There is no other explanation for his unprecedented success. He is unquestionably the best tournament player in the world. But what's more remarkable is that, according to everyone in the know, he is one of only four or five players who have shown long-term profit in the $4,000-$8,000 game. This means that Ivey regularly outplays those with proven talent who have decades of experience to draw upon. There seems to be little question that before his career is over, Ivey will be considered the best who ever played the game.

I can't attempt to define the precise nature of Ivey's talent. He's notoriously private and unforthcoming in interviews. But I feel safe in saying that Ivey is a genius of some sort. One cannot be the best in an intellectual endeavor pursued by millions without possessing a profound intelligence. Whatever the exact nature of Ivey's gifts—whether he's an uncanny observer of human nature or possesses some preternatural ability to recognize patterns—there's little doubt that his skills are transferable. I'd imagine that many with similar gifts make millions on Wall Street or in consulting firms where determining a preferred course of action with incomplete information is an invaluable skill.

But Ivey plays poker. As I watched him at Commerce—his ears covered with massive headphones, his eyes darting from side to side—there was no sense that the game presents any kind of hardship. The ridiculous bad beats, the crushing losses, the dubious company—they're subsumed by his all-engrossing passion for poker.

As I stood watching Ivey, Brunson, Reese, and Greenstein, all of whom have made more than enough money to support their families for at least a couple of generations, I marveled. After all the years of play and all the money they have made, they were here, playing poker. They could be anywhere, doing anything.

So I watched these titans of the game, and I returned to the two simple questions that I had to confront. First, could I beat the games? Clearly the answer was yes. I have the intelligence and spirit that will allow me to profit for years to come. Around the donkeys who seemed almost eager to give away their money at the $10–$20, I could do quite well. I doubt I'd ever be a millionaire, but I'm confident that I could put together a tidy six-figure income for a long time. If I had the endurance, I could compete on the tournament trail.

But then there was the second question: *Do I really want to do this fifty hours a week for decades?* Here the answer was equally clear. No. After only three months of intensive daily play I was tired and frustrated, my mood continually sour. I wanted to be home, with Marisa. I wanted to spend my nights away from casinos, enjoying friends who had normal occupations—teachers, lawyers, bankers. I wanted to watch *The Daily Show* on weekdays and eat leisurely dinners and take in plays on the weekends. I wanted to be in New York. I wanted a family. I wanted a life that was a little closer to normal.

I returned to my table surprisingly pleased with my realization.

It was early still, before 11:00 P.M., and I felt sharp and oddly energized. I chatted up a couple of men at my table who were pretty clearly fish hunters. They were entrenched in their chairs, waiting for the weak and incompetent to stumble by and lose their money. One taught college-level French; the other was an unemployed engineer. I was enjoying the lively company and wasn't worried especially about the few hundred I'd lost. Then I found A♥-K♥ in middle position and made a raise to $100 after an early-position player limped. It was folded back around to the limper, a man in his early forties who wore a golf shirt and a sullen expression. He called.

The flop was 4♥-9♥-J♠. With my heart draw, I liked this flop, so when he checked, I bet $200. He quickly called. The turn brought the A♣. Once again my hand had gone from good to outstanding. When he checked again, I bet $500.

"All-in," he announced in a shot. My heart sank. It would cost me another $1,500 to call. I was nearly certain I was behind. A check-raise after the Ace hit the board was a sign of great strength. A sane person wouldn't make a move like that without two-pair or a set, but I didn't see how I could fold. I had a decent hand with top pair, and there was at least some chance that my opponent was bluffing. What's more, I had the draw. Any heart would give me the nuts.

"Dealer," I said, "please don't put out the river." Then I turned to my opponent and asked, "Do you do business?" I was asking my opponent if he'd like to run the river multiple times. It was a way of stemming some of the risk. If he had two-pair, he'd hate to lose the whole pot if my flush card came. And if we ran the river two or three times, I stood a better chance of getting some of my money back from this very large pot.

"Yeah, I do," he said.

"OK, so what do you have?"

"I'm not showing you my cards."

This made no sense. How could either of us intelligently decide what to do if we had no idea what the other held? I explained the concept, but he was adamant. I was unsure how to proceed but was still fairly certain I had the second-best hand, so I suggested we run the river twice. He agreed.

The first card paired the 4, the second was a 7♦. I'd missed my flush both times and showed my lone pair.

"You're good both times," he said and threw his cards away.

Yet another fish. Yet another successful hunt.

# EPILOGUE

MARISA, SMILING BROADLY, WALKED WITH ME DOWN WEST Broadway just north of Prince Street. The smile had been fixed on her face for a few days, since I gave her the ring that now sits on her left hand. It's a beautiful piece: a platinum band with a shallow, rounded curve. A small diamond sits within the peak of the curve. I bought the ring in L.A., the day after my final poker session. And at the risk of overestimating my taste, I did wonderfully. It's unusual, clearly lacking in heft, but it suits her delicate fingers perfectly.

Marisa was especially joyful that day because we were embarking on an outing that was unprecedented in either of our histories. And Marisa adores new experiences. We were spending the day shopping in trendy, overpriced SoHo stores. I had a speaking engagement in Vegas, and for this trip Marisa was coming with me. Our time in Vegas was well planned: a Cirque du Soleil show, dinner at Eiffel Tower Restaurant, and dancing at one of the many night spots. But before we embarked, we needed suitably extravagant clothes. I was looking forward to spending some of the $31,400 I had made on the trip.

We saw some nice stuff in the first couple of shops we stopped in—faded low-riding jeans that could be paired with silky camisole tops. But neither of us was thrilled with these offerings. I was determined to buy her a dress or a skirt. I figured I saw a lot of Marisa in jeans, and for this night I hoped we could both look a little different.

We stumbled into our fourth store and immediately stopped at a mannequin wearing a flowered skirt and a matching sheer wrap for a top.

"That's nice," she said, her tone deeply appreciative, and I agreed. But the color was wrong for her, a light blue that wouldn't work with her olive Colombian-Italian skin. So we went to the racks looking for other choices. It wasn't long before she found the same combination in a light green. "Ohh," she said softly. Reflexively, she looked at the price tag and shook her head.

"Try it on," I prodded. The outfit was beautiful, and if nothing else, I wanted to see her in it.

We were escorted to the dressing room, where the couch for waiting men was more comfortable than anything I'd ever owned. She stepped out of the dressing room, and we both beamed. She was dazzling, and we both knew it.

She mentioned the price again, and I waved her off. We were buying this. She changed and we moved to the cashier, who expertly folded the garment and told me the tax-adjusted price. I produced a portion of my roll and peeled off the necessary cash. As the cashier moved to get change, Marisa quipped, "I feel like a different kind of woman."

"Yeah, I guess you finally found your sugar daddy," I said. I smiled and placed my hand under her chin and gently tilted her head upward so I could kiss her mouth.

I continued to play high limits for a few weeks after my return, but stopped after hitting a three-day stretch where I lost $11,000. The setback was upsetting, but I didn't lose any sleep. There was no hand-wringing or anxiety. When I looked back at the hands involved, I concluded that I played reasonably well and was the victim of some bad luck.

I never told Marisa about those losses. It was enough for her to know how I was doing in the broadest context—that I had been profitable over the previous months. I was no longer discussing any day's results. When she'd ask how my day had gone, I'd simply say, "Fine." I might discuss a hand that presented an interesting intellectual challenge, but I was keeping the bad beats and the suckouts to myself.

After the big loss, I decided to take a break from poker. I thought the break would last a few days, but it went on for months. I took on demanding contracting work and found no time for long sessions. As I finish this book, a year after completing the trip, I find some time to play—maybe online a couple of days a week, but that is about it. My income is no longer reliant on poker so I no longer called myself a pro or even a semipro.

That's fine with me. I want to write another book and I've got a wedding to plan. I've taken a good deal of my bankroll and applied it toward the wedding. At some point during the reception I'll be sure to toast the fish with the champagne that they've paid for.